- **SECULAR PHILOSOPHY**
- **THE OCCULT**
- **EXTRAMARITAL AFFAIRS**
- **WOMEN'S RIGHTS**
- **CHURCH AND FAMILY AUTHORITY**

Those weren't the hot issues back in Jerusalem.

But when the gospel came to the regions beyond—bustling European cities such as Athens, Corinth, Philippi, and Thessalonica—it was a different story. Paul and his colleagues faced a whole new set of questions . . . questions that sound surprisingly like the twentieth century.

The gospel proved equal to the challenge. It took root and grew in European soil just as it had back in Palestine. And the letters Paul wrote to explain Christ's response to the new issues help us find our way in a turbulent modern society.

THE GRACE CHURCH
P.O. BOX 41
13301 E. DAWSON RD.
LOCKEFORD, CA 95237

*Grace Church of Lockeford*

**Other BIBLE ALIVE titles:**
**OLD TESTAMENT SURVEYS**
Let Day Begin
Freedom Road
Years of Darkness, Days of Glory
Edge of Judgment
Lift High the Torch
Springtime Coming

**NEW TESTAMENT SURVEYS**
The Servant King
The Great Adventure
Christ Preeminent
Pass It On
His Glory

# LARRY RICHARDS
## BIBLE ALIVE SERIES

# Regions Beyond

The Early Church in Mission

Studies in Acts, I and II Thessalonians, I and II Corinthians

David C. Cook Publishing Co.
ELGIN, ILLINOIS—WESTON, ONTARIO
FULLERTON, CALIFORNIA

**REGIONS BEYOND**
© 1977 David C. Cook Publishing Co.

All rights reserved. With the exception of specifically indicated material and brief excerpts for review purposes, no part of this book may be reproduced or used in any form without written permission from the publisher.

Scripture quotations, unless otherwise noted, are from the New International Version.

Published by David C. Cook Publishing Co., 850 N. Grove Ave., Elgin, IL 60120
Edited by Timothy Udd and Dean Merrill

Printed in the United States of America

ISBN 0-89191-091-3

# CONTENTS

| | | |
|---|---|---|
| 1 | To Hope Again *Acts 16–19* | 9 |
| 2 | The Core *Acts 17; 1, 2 Thess.* | 24 |
| 3 | The Personal Touch *1 Thess. 1–2* | 37 |
| 4 | Transformed *1, 2 Thess.* | 49 |
| 5 | One Family, Indivisible *1 Cor. 1–4* | 61 |
| 6 | The Duty to Discipline *1 Cor. 5–6* | 75 |
| 7 | The Right to Be Wrong *1 Cor. 8–10* | 85 |
| 8 | Trouble Over Tongues *1 Cor. 12–14* | 99 |
| 9 | Women in the Church *1 Cor. 7, 11* | 112 |
| 10 | Resurrection! *1 Cor. 15–16* | 127 |
| 11 | The Inadequate Man *2 Cor. 1–4* | 137 |
| 12 | "Life Is at Work in You" *2 Cor. 5–9* | 149 |
| 13 | The Use and Abuse of Authority *2 Cor. 10–13* | 159 |

# REGIONS BEYOND

# 1
*Acts 16–19*

# TO HOPE AGAIN

HOW CAN WE DESCRIBE the early church? Dynamic? Explosive? Vital? Alive?

These are some of the best words to describe how suddenly the gospel exploded out of Palestine to capture the allegiance of hundreds of thousands in the ancient world. Within a few decades, the face of the Roman Empire was significantly changed by the aggressive Christian movement. Confronting an entrenched paganism, the new faith broke down cultural barriers and turned things upside down. Looking back on those vigorous early days, it's easy for us to wish we had lived then and shared the excitement. There was a world to conquer, and the living Spirit of the Church was bent on conquest.

If only we could recapture that sense of mission and purpose.

If only the Church of today were as vital and alive!

## EMPTY LONGING?

All too often when we gaze at the New Testament's portrait of the early church, we visualize something we feel is gone. We compare the Spirit's work in history with our own experience as Christians, and we seem forced to discouraging conclusions. The vitality, the life, the sense of purpose Christ brought then seems lost in modern life. So, to some extent, reliving New Testament times through God's Word may even seem depressing.

But not necessarily. First, the Bible is not just a book of the past. The Bible does not simply describe what God *has done* in His Church; it describes what God *is doing*. The living Word of God, as we'll see in these studies of the Church in mission, describes our own day just as accurately as it describes the first century.

Second, the Bible reveals vital principles as well as historic events. God's goal is to guide *us* to an experience of vitality fully as exciting as in days gone by. A study of the New Testament brings not discouragement but a rebirth of hope. God does not speak to shame us for our deficiencies; He calls us to new experiences.

Third, as we examine the New Testament closely, we are struck again and again with the *similarity* between the issues confronting the early church and those confronting us today. As the similarities become clear, we begin to understand the real challenges of this twentieth century, and we understand—perhaps for the first time—*just how to meet them victoriously.* The nature of the Church of Christ comes into focus. Rediscovering our identity as God's people, we find again the pathway we have lost.

Perhaps as you begin this study, you are satisfied with your Christian experience. Perhaps you don't feel uncertain about the meaning and purpose of your life. Perhaps you do not feel a growing helplessness in light of the breakdown of values in our society. Perhaps you do not share modern man's desperate, restless search for hope.

But if you *do* feel any of these things, then these New Testament studies are most certainly for you. In His living Word, God speaks directly to us in our own world today, and He invites us to move beyond empty longing to a unique recovery of hope.

## CONFRONTATION

For some fifteen years after Jesus' resurrection, the great majority of believers were Hebrew Christians, committed to the traditions and life-style of Israel. Early Christians were looked on as members of a sect within Judaism. Their struggles to define the meaning of the new faith were more or less confined to Judea, one small province on the far frontier of the vast Roman Empire.

These were, of course, important years for the community of faith. The Church made the startling discovery that Israel's Messiah had died and risen again to bring forgiveness to Gentiles as well as to Jews. An important struggle over the relationship between faith and the Law developed, was worked out in a council at Jerusalem, and defined in Paul's subsequent letters to the Galatians and the Romans.

The new faith spread slowly through Jewish communities, taking firm root in Antioch, where the first predominantly Gentile church was formed. Its aggressive nature could be sensed in the first missionary journey of Paul and Barnabas. But during the first decade and a half of its existence, the Church—as far as society as a whole was concerned—was almost an underground movement.

These were years of internal growth and maturing, of gathering strength and deepening commitment. Finally, with the foundation of self-understanding laid, the early church exploded throughout the Roman Empire, challenging the most basic ideas and values of the Roman/Hellenic world!

This world the early church boldly confronted was a world as complex and cosmopolitan as our own. It was composed of many different peoples, each with their own ethnic heritages. Yet, over the centuries since Alexander the Great's military conquests, a number of common bonds had developed. For one thing, while Alexander's political superstructure had shattered, the Hellenistic (Greek) culture he sought to promote had conquered. Hellenistic ideas took root. Greek became the common language of the world. Greek customs, buildings, art, philosophy, and habits of thought pervaded.

REGIONS BEYOND

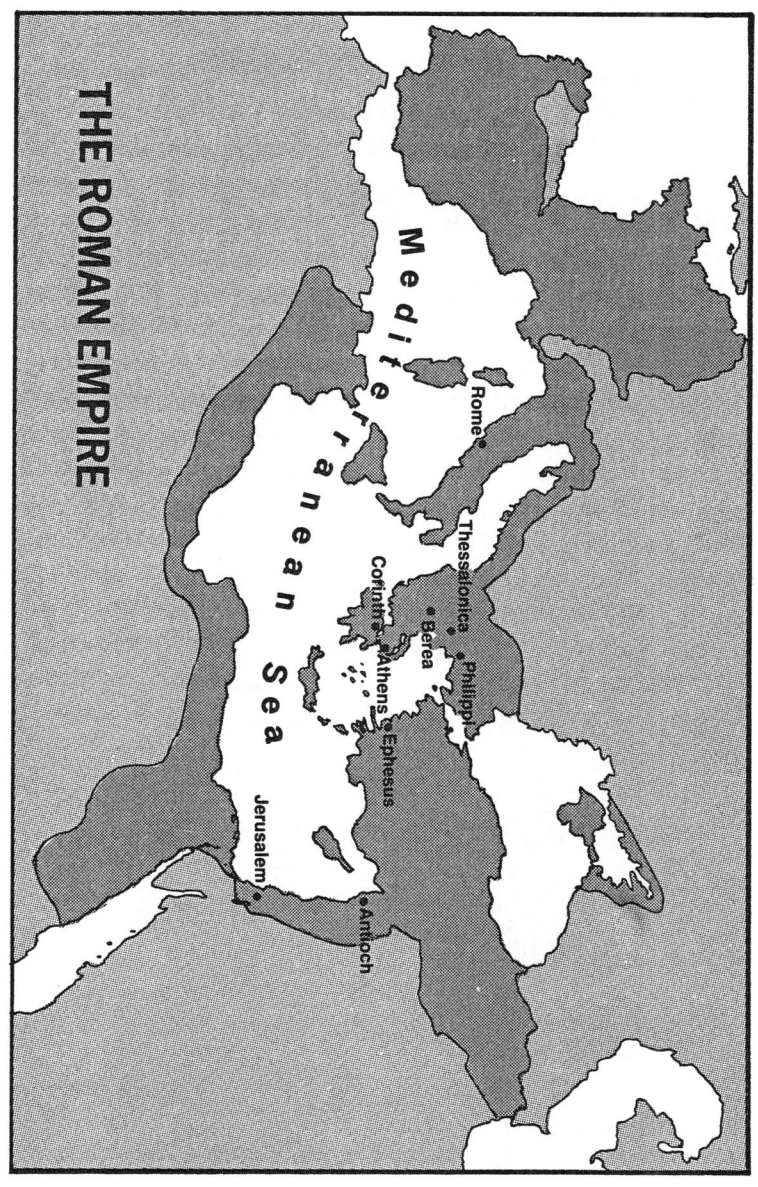

BIBLE ALIVE SERIES

Even the Jews, always fiercely committed to their Law and traditions, were deeply affected. Long before the birth of Christ, the Old Testament had been translated into Greek (this translation is called the Septuagint), because many of the Jews who had settled in the lands beyond Palestine had gradually lost their command of Hebrew and Aramaic.

In religion, in philosophy, in the values that gave shape to life, the Hellenistic culture overcame where the force of Greek arms had failed.

But the political power in the world of the first century was Rome. Military conquest, matched with a practical efficiency in administration, welded the Western world together. Shipping routes were established and protected, roads constructed and maintained. Travel was freely permitted; individual rights were protected. Ideas as well as goods flowed from region to region within the empire. Banking, (with lending and borrowing, letters of credit, discount notes, and accrued interest varying from 4 to 10 percent) was a basic feature of financial life. Trade guilds foreshadowed modern labor unions; medicine and dentistry were relatively advanced; X-rated stage shows were common. Poetry, literature, and music were available, as well as the chariot races—the Indianapolis 500 and LeMans of their day.

Skimming Acts 16—19, which describes that explosive expansion of the early church initiated by Paul's second missionary journey, we gain varied impressions of that world.

*Acts 16:1-5.* Immediately we're introduced to

Timothy, a youth who typified the first-century world. The son of a Jewish mother and a Greek father, Timothy reflected his century's melting-pot quality. Races and cultures united, retaining something of their heritage but also forming something democratic and new.

*Acts 16:11-15.* Luke, the author of Acts, who had joined the missionary company, identifies Philippi as a "Roman colony and the leading city of that district of Macedonia" (v. 12). Originally, Roman colonies were garrison settlements of Roman citizens in captured territories, often populated by army veterans and their families. They had such rights as "autonomous government, freedom from taxation, and the same legal privileges as if they were living in Italy."[1] The crossroads for both sea and land trade routes, Philippi was an important center of business, government, communications, and culture. It was typical of the metropolitan centers that the missionaries chose for church-planting.

Lydia and the women with her were most likely Gentile proselytes (converts) to Judaism. While there was a state religion, which in the West involved emperor worship as well as the worship of the older pantheon of gods and goddesses, Eastern religious cults also had great appeal. It was common for smaller groups of men and/or women to form cult groups. These private religious associations sometimes demanded high moral standards and promised divine compensation for good and bad conduct. Other cultic faiths, the "mystery religions," appealed "to a deep and growing sense of need in the

Hellenistic period for a personal religious experience and future salvation."[2] The mystery religions featured myths and ritual designed to offer hope. In general, they had little moral or ethical content; in fact, at times they were grossly sensual and sexual in emphasis.

So it wasn't surprising in this complex religious climate to find a group of women drawn to Judaism and gathering outside the city for worship. Nor was it surprising to see Paul sit down and informally share the Christian message.

*Acts 16:16-21.* Inside the city, we see another aspect of the religious climate of the Roman world. Paul and the others were followed by a slave girl who "had a spirit by which she predicted the future" (v. 16). As a fortune-teller, she earned a great deal of money for her owners—until Paul, in the name of Jesus, cast out the spirit.

Occultism was a feature of the first-century world just as it is a growing element in our own. Exorcism was well known (Acts 19: 13-16); witchcraft and sorcery were practiced (19: 17-20). Despite the many religions and philosophies, the average man sensed his hopelessness and knew uncertainty and fear. As Merrill Tenney points out, "The pagan world took for granted that men were under the influence of invisible forces of evil which continually sought their destruction. Only by obtaining ascendancy over these powers through magical arts could they retain their freedom."[3]

*Acts 16:35-40.* Jailed in Philippi because of mob violence stimulated by the slave girl's owners, the missionaries were miraculously released. When the magistrates discovered that they had "publicly without a trial" (v. 37) beaten men who were Roman citizens, they quickly came to appease the missionary party. Such official misconduct might have cost them their positions or even severe punishment! Roman justice, including the protection of the rights of the individual, was swift and fair. As today, federal justice superseded state and local systems.

*Acts 17:1-4.* Moving on to Thessalonica, Paul went first to the Jewish synagogue there. In the first-century world there were probably some four million Jews, and less than 20 percent lived in Palestine. Most major cities had colonies of Jewish citizens engaged in trade, banking, or manufacturing. In these Jewish centers the Old Testament faith had been maintained, and some of the Gentile population had been attracted to Judaism. These Gentiles often became "God-fearers," adherents to the moral and theological teachings of Judaism but not full converts to its restrictive life-style.

Such Jewish centers were normally the place where Paul began his mission.

*Acts 17:16-21.* In Athens, Paul was confronted with a city "full of idols" (v. 16) and with philosophers constantly speculating over the nature and meaning of life. Luke notes, "All the Athenians and the foreigners who lived there spent their time doing nothing but talking about and listening to the latest ideas" (v. 21), a rather graphic description that may remind us of today's intelligentsia.

Paul gave the residents of Athens a unique exposition of the gospel, starting from the assumptions and ideas of his listeners and then leading them to a confrontation with revealed truth. His sermon here, so different from Peter's sermons recorded earlier in Acts, "recognizes the philosophical cast of mind of his audience and presents his message understandingly to them in terms of the three great questions of philosophy: 'Whence,' 'What,' and 'Whither'; or otherwise stated, 'the origin,' 'the nature,' and 'the end of all things.' "[4] In his exposition, Paul quoted not from Scripture, but from Greek religious poetry!

*Acts 18:1-5.* Moving on from Athens, Paul came to Corinth, a city that typifies another dimension of the first-century world. *Corinth* was a byword for licentiousness and moral corruption, so much so that "to Corinthianize" was a common phrase meaning "to carry on immorally."

Here Paul lived for some time, teaching in the synagogue until he was expelled, and then teaching in the home of a believer next door to the synagogue.

*Acts 19:8-10.* Moving on to Ephesus, Paul found himself in one of the world's great religious centers. This city's life was dominated by the temple and cult worship of Diana (or Artemis). Here Paul again taught, first in the Jewish synagogue, then, when expelled, in the lecture hall of Tyrannus, who apparently was one of the many teachers of rhetoric or philosophy found in first-century cities. Paul rented his facilities for use when the owner was not teaching.

Within two years, the gospel message had such an impact in the city that the business of the silversmiths and other craftsmen, which was based on selling religious items to tourists and pilgrims, had fallen off significantly. The leader of the tradesmen warned his fellow craftsmen not only of a loss of trade but "also that the temple of the great goddess Artemis will be discredited, and the goddess herself, who is worshiped throughout the province of Asia and the world, will be robbed of her divine majesty" (19:27)!

Again a riot ensued, but this time it was squelched by the city officials, who insisted that the swelling Christian movement "neither robbed temples nor blasphemed our goddess" (19:37). Christianity did confront the culture and faith of the first century, but the confrontation was on the deepest levels of human experience and not marked by disrespectful actions or language.

The Church in mission is neither rebellious nor destructively radical. The Christian revolution takes place within the hearts of men. Confrontations that invariably follow the gospel message are the outgrowth of personal transformation. With the gospel comes a rediscovery of reality and a recovery of hope. And *these* are the key to building the Kingdom of God.

## CONTEXTUALIZATION

Reading Acts 16—19 carefully, we're struck by a missionary approach very unlike the "Church militant" picture that is often drawn. There is no attacking of the institutions of society. Instead, there seems to be an almost shocking *accommodation* to societal institutions and mores.

Paul had Timothy circumcised "because of the Jews who lived in that area, for they all knew that his father was a Greek" (16: 3). In Philippi, days went by before Paul finally exorcised the spirit from the slave girl who followed him, even though this "endorsement" by a local witch might well have been misunderstood. In Philippi, too, Paul insisted on his rights as a Roman citizen. Somehow his citizenship in heaven did not lead him to insist on full separation between church and state! In Athens Paul deserted the usual approach of appeal to the Old Testament to accommodate himself to the approach of philosophic discourse, even to the extent of quoting from pagan religious poets rather than the inspired Word (17: 22-34). In Ephesus he held classes in the local school of philosophy, even adopting its form ("discussions," 19: 9). There the subsequent impact of the gospel came indirectly: those who burned their books on sorcery and those who stopped purchasing the religious items from the local shops did so because something had happened within them and not, as the city clerk testified, because of any campaign mounted against paganism.

In significant ways the missionaries apparently *attempted to make the gospel fit in the first-century world.*

Today in modern missions, much concern is being given to what is called *contextualization* of the gospel message. It's clear that some of the things we associate with the Christian faith (such as the 11:00 A.M. worship service on Sunday) are artifacts of Western culture and have nothing to do with the content of the gospel itself. Also, it is obvious that while we must constantly affirm and teach the core content of the gospel, aspects of Christianity that reflect a particular society's way of practicing the faith must not be confused with the gospel core. In fact, God seeks to work through His Word to build His Church in many varying cultures, and the church in one setting may well have significant differences from the church in another. Paul's approach to mission and his adaptability to different groups and situations help us remember that we, too, must never confuse the form with content.

Perhaps this is one reason why some Christians today do not have the sense of hope and purpose that shines through the New Testament documents. Perhaps we've become too accustomed to viewing externals as "true Christianity," mistaking our rituals, traditions, and entrenched ways of thought for the underlying realities.

If so, we're about to recover perspective. For the New Testament passages we'll be studying in this book bring us face to face with a world unbelievably like our own.

## GOING DEEPER

*to personalize*

1. Read Acts 16—19 rapidly. When you're finished, jot down your major impressions. Would

you like to have been a Christian then? Why, or why not?

2. Read Acts 16—19 more carefully. List as many similarities between the first-century world and our own as you can find. (A number of them are suggested in this text, pp. 12-18.)

3. In this chapter the author suggests a number of reasons why this study of the New Testament church's early days in mission can be personally meaningful to you (see especially pp. 10, 11, 19-21). Which of these seems most important to you?

4. Write a brief paragraph on "What I hope to gain from this study in the New Testament."

*to probe*

1. The sketch in this chapter and the next of the Hellenistic culture in the early Roman Empire is necessarily brief and superficial. Check a public library for books on the Hellenistic period. Or, read whatever you can find in your church or school library about New Testament times.

Write a brief summary of what you feel are the most significant features.

2. Contextualization of the gospel is briefly described on pages 19-21 of this chapter. Check missions resource libraries for information on this increasingly significant concept, and write a brief paper summarizing issues raised. *Or,* make lists dividing the features of American Christianity between *core* and *cultural* matters. For instance, in which list would you put the following: attitudes toward smoking, courtship practices, church roles

for women, church membership requirements, Sunday school?

   1. Charles W. Carter and Ralph Earle, *The Acts of the Apostles—A Commentary* (Grand Rapids: Zondervan, 1973), p. 232.
   2. Merrill C. Tenney, ed., *The Zondervan Pictorial Encyclopedia of the Bible*, 5 vols. (Grand Rapids: Zondervan, 1974), 4:330.
   3. Merrill C. Tenney, *New Testament Times* (Grand Rapids: Eerdmans, 1965), p. 122.
   4. Carter and Earle, *Acts*, p. 259.

# 2

*Acts 17; 1, 2 Thessalonians*

# THE CORE

IT'S CLEAR FROM OUR READING of Acts 16—19 that the apostle Paul was sensitive to first-century culture. But it should also be clear that Paul was careful never to compromise the core issues of the Christian faith.

The distinction is often lost. It's so easy to take a practice sanctified by tradition and mistake it for a core issue.

For instance, for many years in the United States, Sunday evening was dedicated to evangelistic church services. Non-Christians could be brought to church, and an evangelistic message and invitation became the expected thing. As American society changed and new recreational and entertainment patterns developed, Sunday evening no longer was a time when the unchurched slipped into the pew. Even the annual "revival" was now attended primarily by believers. Yet, the approach of many churches to evangelism continued to be the Sunday evening or special revival service. A "gospel message" was expected, even though the gospel might be familiar to everyone present.

How different this picture is from Acts. There Paul took the gospel where people were, and he adapted the form of presentation to his listeners. We see Paul searching out a riverside place of worship and sitting down to talk the gospel over with Lydia and her friends. We see Paul moving into the synagogue and there debating in the classic way from the Old Testament Scriptures. When Paul stood before the philosophers in Athens, his presentation took the form of philosophic argument, using even pagan religious poetry and an Athenian altar to "An Unknown God" as points of contact. His presentation never once referred to Scripture! In Ephesus we see Paul in the lecture hall of Tyrannus, holding "discussions daily" (19: 9) like other itinerant teachers of his day.

As Paul moved to different settings and different cultures, he *adapted*. He easily shifted the location and even the form of the gospel presentation to fit patterns his listeners were most likely to recognize and understand.

Perhaps, instead of decrying the resistance of men and women to our evangelistic services, to our visitation, or to our presentations of how to be saved, we would do well to recover the cultural sensitivity of the early missionaries. Perhaps then we'd discover that the gospel has not lost its power at all, but that maybe our ways of presenting the gospel and our rigid terminology have, in fact, so insulated the Good News that those we speak to cannot even recognize it!

## FORM AND CONTENT

It's important to realize that, while Paul clearly reshaped the form of his gospel presentation to fit the listener and culture, he did *not* compromise the core itself. D. R. Jackson notes that he spoke "in the way most appropriate to his hearers' circumstances and cultural background,"[1] but that certain basic themes are consistently present. The themes Jackson suggests are: (1) Christ's death, (2) Christ's resurrection, (3) witness testimony, (4) Scripture testimony, (5) power, and (6) forgiveness.

Wherever the gospel message was preached to Jews or others who had a background in the Old Testament, these elements were emphasized. But in the Acts 17 report of Paul's speech to the philosophers of Athens, the proclamation went further.

Paul began in Athens by affirming the existence of a "God who made the world and everything in it" (17:24), who is Himself the sole source of the material universe and animate life. This God who made the world has both design and purpose in His creation. The ages are moving toward a divinely determined end, an end in which God "will judge the world with justice" (17:31). The proof of God's reality and His concern for mankind lies in the fact that God Himself entered space and time in human form, undergoing death and then experiencing a bodily resurrection from the dead (see 17:31)!

Here we have true confrontation with the first-century world. Paul might have adapted the cultural forms for those to whom he spoke, but there was no compromise of the gospel message. And that message went against the grain of the basic beliefs and values of Paul's listeners just as biblical Christianity contradicts the beliefs and values of modern man today.

*A weary world view.* Acts 17 mentions the two prevalent schools of philosophy in the time of the early church: Epicureanism and Stoicism. While differing from each other, both philosophies had the same practical purpose: to find peace of mind. Stoics saw man as a rational being, felt the world had a moral order, and emphasized a kind of universal law that pantheistically pervaded the universe. Epicureans saw man as a feeling being, emphasized the supremacy of the individual, and affirmed that the universe was but a random combination of atoms mechanistically determined. They maintained that seeking pleasurable experience was the best way of life.

Neither philosophy had any place for a divine creation. One viewed matter as eternal, while the other regarded it as pervaded by and essentially equivalent to the divine. Without a personal, supreme God who created for His own purposes, the universe had no known origin, and history had no direction or goal. An individual's relationship to either the universe or God (such a god as there was) had no meaning beyond its own existence; no purpose for life could be found outside the brief span of years allotted to an individual.

To someone seeking the meaning of human existence these ancient philosophies could only say, "Exist!" (Eat, drink, and be merry) or "Endure."

It is true that very few first-century men were philosophers, just as relatively few people of our own day consciously struggle with basic questions. But the emptiness of the current philosophies was reflected in the attitudes and ideas of the general population.

Even the old faith had no adequate explanations. The pantheons of ancient gods and goddesses were simply immortal men and women, freed to indulge in the sins and pettiness their worshipers yearned for themselves. These gods and goddesses had no real concern for humans. Oh, they might choose to favor a special hero such as Achilles or Hercules for a time. But they would capriciously turn away from him on a whim at any moment, or they might make him a pawn in a battle with some rival. What's more, the gods themselves were not all-powerful. Like men, they, too, were helpless before an awesome and impersonal Fate. The average person caught under the crushing weight of chance, helpless to affect the course of his own life, and without any hope of establishing a relationship with a trustworthy supernatural power, had only superstitious ritual or magic practice with which to ward off evil.

Even the mystery religions, which attracted many in the first century, offered, at most, some revival of life in the underworld, an escape from punishment or from continued imprisonment in a succession of bodies (reincarnation). The concept of a conscious, bodily resurrection in space and time was unthinkable.

The view of reality in the ancient world was characterized by these elements:
- an impersonal universe
- an impersonal Fate
- an essential purposelessness
- no hope of a relationship with a faithful deity

Within the framework of this common belief, man lived out his life. The life-style of the age had gradually lost the optimism of early Greek culture (c. 400 B.C.) and had been marred by:
- pluralism (with many competing philosophies of life advanced)
- relativism (with each individual choosing his or her own thing, accepting the idea that what might be "right for me" might not be "right for you")
- superstition (with a variety of straws grasped at in the hope of finding something to satisfy)
- syncretism (with religious and philosophical notions from many sources combined and recombined in an effort to find meaning)

Captured in a world they did not understand, men and women lived lives of quiet desperation or hilarious hopelessness. In the words of Paul, they existed "separate from Christ, excluded from citizenship in Israel and foreigners to the covenants of the promise, without hope and without God in the world" (Eph. 2:12). In the fullest meaning of the word, the first-century world was *lost,* wandering in meaningless illusion, never penetrating to the reality underlying the universe, and never knowing a God exists who offers man a relationship through which he can recover both meaning and hope.

No wonder it was a weary world that the early missionaries invaded! And no wonder that when we look beyond the surface—beyond the peace and prosperity, the often unbridled sensuality, the accomplishments of culture—we find a world of men and women desperately ready for the gospel's good news.

*And today?* How like the first century our day is! With all its material prosperity, our age is marked with a sense of weariness and hopelessness. Disillusioned by the unfulfilled vision of scientific conquests as well as by the patriot's dream, more and more turn to ancient avenues in search of hope. For most men and women, the universe today is as impersonal as it seemed in the first century. With sophistication we explain origins by an evolution that supposedly took place by random chance, bringing life from lifeless matter. From this empty, impersonal origin we seem to move toward a meaningless end. If that end doesn't come soon through a destructive atomic war, mindless depletion of earth's natural resources, overpopulation, or pollution of the environment, then the end will still come in some distant age when the universe itself runs down, the stars wink out, and an endless dark descends.

No wonder that within such an impersonal universe men and women increasingly turn to drugs, to hedonistic sensualism, to astrology, to the occult, or to modern mystery faiths from the East in a desperate search for meaning and for hope.

For perhaps the first time in centuries, the world view of modern man closely resembles the world view of New Testament times! The revolutionary truths so familiar to the Christian are truly revolutionary again. Returning again to the gospel core, you and I are invited by a living Word to experience again the exciting days of the first century when the Church was vital and the faith was young.

CORE TRUTH
*1, 2 Thessalonians*

We know from Acts that Paul did not stay long in Thessalonica. The disturbance described in Acts 17 forced the missionaries out of the city; later attempts by Paul to return were blocked (1 Thess. 2:17, 18). Yet, looking at these two early missionary letters, we see how quickly Paul communicated core truth to new converts and the impact that truth had. "You became imitators of us and of the Lord," Paul reminds his Thessalonian readers. "The Lord's message rang out from you . . . your faith in God has become known everywhere . . . how you turned to God from idols to serve the living and true God, and to wait for his Son from heaven, whom he raised from the dead—Jesus, who rescues us from the coming wrath" (1 Thess. 1:6-10).

Paul clearly points up here the reorientation of life that came when people in the first century grasped the meaning of the gospel's core:
- A personal God lives.
- The God behind the universe calls us to know and serve Him.
- This God invaded history in the person of His Son, and through His Son's historical death and resurrection God rescues us from the coming judgment.
- Jesus' return testifies to the promise that the universe has an end as well as a beginning.

Within the framework of the gospel's glowing revelation of reality, individuals could once again find meaning, purpose, and joy. The underlying reality is God Himself. The life-transforming fact is that this God calls us into a personal relationship with Himself!

We get a clearer impression of Paul's view of core truth through Charles Horne's discussion of the doctrines referred to in the two Thessalonian letters:

> First, as respects the doctrine of God, Paul indicates that there is one true God (I Thes. 1:9). From this one true and living God the Gospel is derived (I Thes. 2:2). To Him they submit themselves for approval of their labor (I Thes. 2:4, 10). He providentially directs their lives (I Thes. 3:11), and He is the one who will perfect the Thessalonians at the coming of Christ (I Thes. 5:23). He has both chosen them (I Thes. 2:4) and is even now calling them unto His own king-

dom and glory (I Thes. 2:12). And this God is faithful; He will accomplish the work which He has begun (I Thes. 5:24).

Second, as respects the doctrine of Christ, the apostle so unites the Son with the Father that their essential unity is indicated (I Thes. 1:1). He is described as "the Lord," the common term for God among the Jews of this time.

Third, as respects the doctrine of the Holy Spirit, the apostle teaches that it is the Spirit who makes the message effective in the hearts of hearers (I Thes. 1:5). The Spirit gives joy in affliction (I Thes. 1:6); the Spirit calls believers to a holiness like His own (I Thes. 1:7)....

Fifth, as respects the doctrine of eschatology, the apostle has considerable to set forth. From the futuristic perspective the "obtaining of salvation" is principally conceived in the Thessalonian epistles (I Thes. 5:9; II Thes. 2:14). The basic emphasis theologically in the Thessalonian epistles is eschatological. The definite announcement of the Second Coming rounds off each step in the apostolic argument.[2]

The new converts had been firmly grounded in core truth. A new view of reality, penetrating beyond the mists of illusion and empty human reasoning to the Person who made the universe for His own good and loving purposes, literally revolutionized the lives of first-century people.

With the rediscovery of reality, they experienced a joyful recovery of hope. And the Church exploded to sweep victoriously through the Western world.

**BIBLE ALIVE SERIES**

## GOING DEEPER
*to personalize*

1. The author in pages 27-30 sketches the concept of the universe characteristic in the first century. Can you think of evidence to support or to cast doubt on his suggestion that today, too, most people assume that the universe is essentially impersonal and that human life is essentially meaningless?

List all the evidence you can think of on either side. (For instance, what is the tone of contemporary literature and theater?)

2. To what extent do you think Christians have adopted the attitudes and values of the world around them, even though they may have a different belief about the nature of the universe and the reality of God?

3. Do your own careful study of 1 and 2 Thessalonians. Underline in your Bible those verses or phrases that seem to you to present core truth (that is, those that make distinctive statements about the nature of the universe, the future, God, and God's relationship with man or history).

After you have finished your study and your underlining, *write* a summary of "The Biblical Portrait of Reality."

4. In the first century it was common practice to "dispose of" unwanted babies. Girl children in particular were often simply placed on the nearest rubbish heap at birth to die of exposure to the elements. Early census figures indicate that even well-to-do families seldom chose to raise more than one daughter.

Can you see any relationship between this practice and the then prevalent societal view of reality?

What about today's growing acceptance of abortion "on demand" for the mother's convenience? What view of life and its meaning does the proabortion position seem to imply?

5. Look again at the list of core truths you found in the Thessalonian letters. If nominal Christians today seriously believed them, what changes might you expect in their lives? List at least five.

*to probe*

In this chapter the author notes that the early missionaries felt free to adapt their presentation of the gospel message to fit their hearers' background and ways of thinking. But, within this context, they were careful not to compromise the gospel core.

Thinking about our own culture and society as you know it, which of the following approaches to evangelism do you feel would be appropriate today? For each approach you do *not* feel "fits" today's world, think of a better one to reach the desired audience:

1. Passing out tracts on the street corner
2. Holding revival meetings in a church building
3. Putting evangelistic sermons on TV
4. Holding a debate on a college campus
5. Busing children to Sunday school
6. Holding Bible studies in a living room
7. Doing house-to-house visitation using the Four Spiritual Laws

8. Offering marriage counseling free to members of the community
9. Encouraging the organization of a mayor's prayer breakfast

Be sure you list reasons why each approach does or does not fit contemporary culture as well as reasons why your alternative approaches might!

1. *Zondervan Pictorial Encyclopedia,* 5:725.
2. *Zondervan Pictorial Encyclopedia,* 5:725.

# 3

*1 Thessalonians 1, 2*

# THE PERSONAL TOUCH

IT WOULD BE A MISTAKE to believe that the New Testament church captured the first-century world by the power of a "better idea."

Paul did not preach a new philosophy.

The response was, at heart, a response to the personal God who, in Jesus, offers forgiveness and an endless relationship with Himself. That is the gospel's real power.

In the first century, the revelation of God as the person who loves came as a jolting surprise. W. W. Tarn, in his book on Hellenistic civilization, notes that two vital elements in the new religion, quite apart from the figure of the Founder, had no counterpart in Hellenistic thought. The first was the revelation of personal immortality and resurrection. The second was the fact that

> of all the Hellenistic creeds, none was based on love of humanity; none had any message for the poor and the wretched, the publican and the sinner. Those who

laboured and were heavy laden were to welcome a different hope from any which Hellenism could offer.[1]

The mystery cults might offer initiates a mystical association. Help might be given in case of illness or with burial costs. But cult members were not family. Their god or goddess did not love them, nor were the initiate's brothers and sisters bound together in a mutual commitment of love for one another.

And then the gospel message came.

God loved them.

Christ died for them, according to the Scriptures.

God called them to receive forgiveness of sins, and to become a member of His family *forever*.

Now, as then, *God wants to establish a permanent personal relationship with you.*

It was the personal dimension of the gospel message, even more than its core truth about reality, that captured hearts. When Paul addressed the Thessalonians in his first letter and said, "Brothers loved by God, we know that he has chosen you" (1:4), he was striking a totally new cord.

"Brothers."

"Loved by God."

"Chosen."

It was the assurance of God's love, made known at last in Jesus, that filled the early church with joy, gave the early missionaries their boundless confidence, and motivated the great outreach movement to take the gospel to each man's neighbors and to the regions beyond.

How do we communicate the love of God?
How does the New Testament indicate that we are to communicate *relationship?*

## COMMUNICATING LOVE

These are important questions. All too often truth is communicated *without* love. All too often beliefs are presented as though they were independent of relationship.

- Imagine a faithful churchman, orthodox in belief. If he fails to realize that true Christianity involves establishing a personal relationship with God, orthodoxy will become empty and meaningless.
- Imagine a person evangelized by a stranger who comes to her door. In five minutes, after a patterned, step-by-step presentation of gospel facts, she is urged to make a commitment to Christ. What has been communicated? The reality of a relationship? A system of beliefs? What?
- Imagine a Christian who builds walls between himself and the non-Christians around him, coming out from behind only to invite the others to church or to some evangelistic study group or rally. What impression of Christianity will he give? Will his attempts at communicating Christian beliefs give adequate expression to the reality of God's love? Will he communicate a gospel relationship?

What is important to see in the New Testament documents is that in the early church *the reality of relationship with God shone through.* The Church comes alive in any age when truth and love find a balanced expression. Through the experience of truth and love, our church of the twentieth century can come alive as well.

First Thessalonians 1 and 2 are chapters we want to restudy because they give us such a clear picture of how love is communicated.

*The Thessalonian letters.* Paul and his companions had gone to Thessalonica early in his second missionary journey (about A.D. 49). Acts 17 tells us that he first approached the Jewish community and for three Sabbaths presented the gospel. It's likely that he stayed in this Greek city for up to six months, until finally the Jews marshaled opposition and expelled him. Thus the Christian church there was largely composed of Gentiles (1 Thess. 1:9; 2:14; Acts 17:4).

Thessalonica, as was typical of the cities in which Paul chose to found new churches, was located on the main highway from east to west, had a good harbor, and was a center of trade. It was also the largest and most important city in Macedonia, and its capital.

The church founded there was a vigorous one; it grew rapidly, both in size and in commitment. Paul says, "You became a model to all the believers in Macedonia and Achaia," and that "the Lord's message rang out from you not only in Macedonia and Achaia—your faith in God has become known everywhere" (1 Thess. 1:7, 8). Since this letter was written in A.D. 50 or 51, it is clear that the gospel not only took root quickly but also that within a very short time this new church moved out aggressively to plant new churches throughout the province of Macedonia.

Paul not only had succeeded in communicating God's love and the reality of a personal relationship with Jesus, but he had somehow equipped the new believers to communicate that relationship to others. Perhaps this is what Paul means in chapter 1 when he writes, "You became imitators of us and of the Lord" (v. 6). Turning from their empty idols, they joyfully committed themselves to know and to serve the "living and true God" and were willing "to wait for his Son from heaven" (1: 9, 10). These new believers embraced both the relationship and the content of the gospel.

*Reality.* Looking at 1 Thessalonians 2, we begin to see how Paul and others in the first-century church communicated the reality of the gospel relationship. The means is so simple and so obvious that we might tend to overlook it when we read this epistle. Yet, it rests on a profound and basic principle.

The Scriptures claim to reveal the truth about life and its meaning. We're told in its core truths about a God who created the universe in which we live. We're told that He created man in His own image, and that even though man sinned, God determined to redeem him. We're told that one day Jesus, who was born into the real world, who lived and died here and was resurrected bodily and ascended into heaven, where He now is with the Father, will one day return in triumph. The great questions about the origin, the meaning, and the goal of the universe are given a distinctive and positive answer. We're told that this is an accurate description of reality, that one day we will be present when God's Son returns from heaven. Then we'll *know*, because we will participate in that great final denouement.

*But we must take all these affirmations on faith. We cannot test these realities personally.* We cannot experience them directly now. The core truths of the gospel *are* true. And we believe them. But we cannot experientially test them.

However, the gospel also presents relational truth. The Bible affirms that God loves us and that, to Him, each person is a precious and valuable individual, worth even the ultimate sacrifice. The Bible claims that when you and I respond to Jesus, God draws us into His family; we become His sons and daughters, and we become brothers and sisters in a new and loving community.

This gospel truth is also presented as reality. And this reality can be experienced now! We *can* test it experientially! *We can know the love of God as He loves us through His family.*

This theme occurs so often in Scripture that it's hard to see how we sometimes miss it. "Christ's love compels us," Paul told the Corinthians (2 Cor. 5:14). "You are a letter from Christ," he explained, "written not with ink but with the Spirit of the living God, not on tablets of stone but on tablets of human hearts" (3:3). The living personality of the Christian becomes the message as God writes His own character and personality on us!

No wonder Jesus gave us the new commandment

to "love each other as I have loved you" (John 15:12). With the command He gave this promise: "All men will know that you are my disciples if you love one another" (John 13:35). *The reality of the love of God is communicated in our love,* both for one another and for the lost for whom Christ died.

The gospel claims about relationship are testable. And the test of that reality is love.

*The pattern.* First Thessalonians 2, and particularly verses 7 through 12, give us a picture of the intimate relationships that characterized Paul's ministry in the new church. The picture is all the more striking when we realize how short a time Paul had spent with them.

> We were gentle among you, like a mother caring for her little children. We loved you so much that we were delighted to share with you not only the gospel of God but our lives as well, because you had become so dear to us.
>
> Surely you remember, brothers, our toil and hardship; we worked night and day in order not to be a burden to anyone while we preached the gospel of God to you.
>
> You are witnesses, and so is God, of how holy, righteous and blameless we were among you who believed. For you know that we dealt with each of you as a father deals with his own children, encouraging, comforting and urging you to live lives worthy of God, who calls you into his kingdom and glory.

A stranger might come to town and propound new doctrines in order to gain a following. In the New Testament world, it was expected that such an itinerant teacher would come, make a living on the fees he charged his disciples, and then move on. But no passing philosopher or proselytizer would ever arrive, undergo hardships to support himself, and actually *love* those whom he taught! No one had ever before shared *himself* as well as his philosophy. No one had ever spoken of a father-child relationship with a loving God and then gone on to actually treat his disciples with that same tender family love he insisted God offers.

Paul's communication of the gospel characteristically involved building a personal relationship with new believers in which the reality of God's love would be experienced now.

How do we communicate the gospel relationship?

By building personal relationships with others.

How do we communicate God's love?

By loving. And, in loving, letting God love others through us.

## TRUTH AND LOVE

The dynamic church of the New Testament—as well as the dynamic church of every age—is a church in which the twin thrusts of truth and love are understood and kept in balance. Just as there is a place in evangelism for the presentation of core truths—a varied presentation that fits the forms appropriate to the culture—so there is a place in evangelism for communicating the love of God through building personal, loving relationships with others.

It's the same in our experience with one another. There's a place in the life of the Christian community for teaching and explaining distinctive biblical truths that are to shape our understanding of reality. Truth, belief, doctrine—all are an integral part of Christian faith. But there must also be a place in the life of the Christian community for the experiencing distinctive biblical relationships. Real love, real caring, involvement in one another's lives, and that commitment to one another that can be summed up in the word *family* is just as essential. Love, like truth, is an integral part of Christian faith.

*Ministry.* Our insight into the relationship between truth and love helps us better understand how God uses human beings not only to share the gospel but also to nurture others in the faith.

Basically, we minister by word and by example. As any Bible truth is taught, the teacher has the privilege of communicating the reality of that truth through his own life-style. Do we say that forgiveness is God's way of dealing with us? Then we can communicate that reality both by extending forgiveness freely and by accepting forgiveness gratefully when we're to blame. Do we say with the apostle Peter that "all these things shall be dissolved ... with fervent heat" (2 Pet. 3:11-12, KJV), that the material universe is temporary and relatively unimportant? Then we have the privilege of demonstrating that reality by our own lack of materialism—our willingness to give or lend, our freedom in decision making to trust God even when His will involves risk. When as Christians we actually live by the truths we believe, *then* we're able to communicate in compelling ways the truths of the Word.

In his letter to the Philippians, Paul helps us put this concept in perspective. "Whatever you have learned or received or heard from me, or seen in me—put it into practice. And the God of peace will be with you" (4:9). Christian communication involves *content* ("learned or received"), it involves *example* ("heard . . . or seen in me"), and it involves *personal response* on the part of the hearer ("put it into practice"). Then the reality, God, will be known: "The God who gives us peace" (Phil. 4:9, GNB) will be with you. Each element is important. We need the Word. We need the experience of seeing the Word lived out in another person. We ourselves need to respond and to act on God's truth.

All too often in the contemporary church we have stressed two of these elements and overlooked the third. "Hear the Word," we say, "and put it into practice." But we forget that the bridge between hearing and doing is to see reality in another person's life.

### CHRISTIAN COMMUNICATION

| Truth | Living Example | Acted On |
|---|---|---|
| "learned and received" | "heard and seen in me" | "put into practice" |

"And the God of peace will be with you."

REGIONS BEYOND

In the twentieth century we live in a world significantly like the first century. The Church of Jesus Christ is surging toward another dynamic explosion. And we *will* explode. We will know again the excitement, the challenge, the fulfillment, the vitality, and, above all, the taste of Holy Spirit power that rocked the ancient world. We will know them all as God teaches us again to lay firm hold on the truth—and the love—that can bring the recovery of hope to all men.

## GOING DEEPER

*to personalize*

1. Read 1 Thessalonians through carefully. This time, underline all references to the relationship between Paul and the Thessalonian Christians. From your discoveries, *write* an answer to *one* of these questions:
   (a) If you were a new believer in Thessalonica, how would you know Paul loved *you?*
   (b) Describe ways you might demonstrate love to a non-Christian friend and thus communicate the relational dimension of the gospel.
   (c) How in a modern local church might this kind of love find expression? List at least twenty practical ways in which members might "love one another."

2. Look back again in 1 Thessalonians at passages you underlined for 1 above. Which core truths was Paul exemplifying for the new converts, according to these passages?

3. Go back over the list of nine "approaches to evangelism" found under *probe* on pages 35-36. Last week you evaluated them as to their appropriateness for communicating core truth content. This time evaluate the *relational implications* of each. How does each context make it easier or harder to communicate love?

*to probe*
1. Research the role of *love* in the Christian experience. You might begin by looking in a concordance to see how many times the word appears in the New Testament. How often is it used of God's love for us? How often of our love for God? How often of our love for one another? If you want to go on, examine the references in this third category, and summarize what the Bible teaches. How important does love seem to be in the communication of faith? What are the key functions of love? Why is it important? How is love expressed?
2. Research the idea of example or leadership by modeling. Check words like *imitate, example,* and *follow*. Or, read 1 and 2 Timothy, in which Paul writes advice to a young minister. What seems to be the role given to the living example in these books?
Summarize your findings in a short paper.

1. W. W. Tarn, *Hellenistic Civilization* (London: Edward Arnold, 1947), p. 287.

# 4
*1, 2 Thessalonians*

# TRANSFORMED

THE THESSALONIAN LETTERS were written within two years of Paul's first contact with those people. In these letters we see vital aspects of gospel communication. Core truth is presented, but always in the framework of *relationship*. That relationship, rooted in God's love, is demonstrated in the love of believers for one another and for the lost.

The vitality of the Church in any age rests on these factors. And one more: transformation. Grasping these key principles and seeing clearly these critical dimensions for our own lives today will lead to a recovery of our hope.

Truth.

Love.

Transformation.

All are realities of the life in Christ on which you and I can build.

BIBLE ALIVE SERIES

## ALL NEW

Hellenistic religions and philosophies did have moral content. Some were highly ethical and proposed strict standards, while others seemed actually to foster immorality. But none gave the believer any real hope.

Then the message of Jesus broke out on the world with the promise that not only would believers have a new relationship with God, but they would also become new and different persons as well! Christianity provided more than a new standard of righteousness. Christianity promised the power to *become* righteous. True to this promise, believers began to experience a progressive transformation that touched every dimension of their personalities. "Your faith is growing more and more, and the love every one of you has for each other is increasing," Paul wrote in his second letter to the Thessalonians (1:3). The capacity to trust and the freedom to love were increasingly characteristic of these young believers. God was working an inner transformation.

Looking again through the Thessalonian epistles, we gain a clear impression of the extent of the transformation that Christianity promises.

*Anxiety and fear* marred many lives, then as now. Increasingly the Thessalonians were able to act in faith, trusting not only God but one another (1 Thess. 1:3, 10; 2 Thess. 1:3, 4). Even when suffering affliction, these men and women were able to retain their confidence (3:4).

*Isolation* was as much a characteristic of first-century life as our own. Individualism created the lonely crowd then as now. But when Christ entered a person's life, this changed. Increasingly the new believers developed the capacity to care. As a result, they reached out in love to others, and others drew close to them as well. Barriers between persons of differing cultures were breached as Christ's transforming power brought a new freedom to love (1 Thess. 1:3; 2:7-11; 3:6-10, 12; 4:9-10; 5:13; 2 Thess. 1:3; 3:5). Love for God and man became a reality.

*Moral compromise* was replaced by steadfastness and commitment. The courage to live by inner convictions, unswayed by circumstance, developed naturally with growth in the new faith (1 Thess. 1:3; 2:14; 3:4, 8; 2 Thess. 1:4).

*Motivations* also underwent an increasingly dramatic change. The self-interest, materialism, natural drives, and passions that once controlled thoughts and actions were replaced by new values and desires (1 Thess. 1:6; 2:4-6, 14, 16; 3:3; 4:3-6, 11-12; 5:8, 12; 2 Thess. 3:6-9). The very core of the personality underwent a gradual transformation as believers experienced more and more of the power of Jesus Christ.

*Personal failures,* an inability to be what they wanted to be, must have nagged first-century men and women even as they do us. But disappointment and shame were gradually replaced, too, as believers discovered a new power for holiness. God's transformation worked within to make these growing believers more and more like Him (1 Thess. 3:12;

4:1, 3, 7; 5:23; 2 Thess. 1:11, 12; 2:13).

*Goallessness and meaninglessness* plagued many lives. With Christ, even this changed. The letters to Thessalonica show us that a new sense of purpose and meaning in life, which could be expressed practically in daily life, began to grip the believers. A commitment to good deeds, to honest work, and to right behavior took on a fresh and deeper meaning as Christians recognized that every action could reflect credit on their Lord (1 Thess. 4:1, 11-12; 5:14-15; 2 Thess. 1:11; 2:17; 3:6-12). Daily duties as well as the privilege of serving others began to bring new satisfaction.

The newness to life did not come from improved circumstances or sudden prosperity. The newness of these Christians' lives was deeply rooted within the believers' own personalities. The fulfilled promise of transformation within is part of the secret of the early church's power. For the first time, such words as "Do not conform any longer to the pattern of this world, but be transformed" (Rom. 12:2) lost all tinge of mockery and brought a living hope.

That hope is ours today, our heritage in the gospel.

## TRANSFORMATION TOOLS

Transformation is not automatic. It wasn't in New Testament times, and it's not today. But transformation is uniquely provided in the Holy Spirit's working through distinctive resources closely associated with the Word.

We saw in the last chapter that God communicates His truths through human models. The written Word and the living example combine to communicate God's truth as reality, not just as concepts or beliefs. This theme is repeated often in the Thessalonian letters (1 Thess. 1:6, 7; 2:14; 4:1; 2 Thess. 3:7-9), and it underlies the power of God's agency for transformation: the Church.

It's important to remember that *church* in the New Testament has an uncluttered meaning. Today we commonly associate the term with a building, Sunday morning services, or an organization with membership, officers, programs, and planned activities. None of these ideas were characteristic of the church of New Testament times. At that time, *church* meant something basic and clear, namely, *community*. The church was an assembly of people, called out of the world into the closest of all possible relationships. The church was and is the family of God.

Thus *church* in the Scripture is a *relational* term. Always in view are the people, who share a common relationship with one Father and with one another as brothers and sisters. In the intimate context of family relationships, God chooses to work His transformation in human lives.

*Socialization.* We all realize the human family is the center of socialization. It's here that personality is originally shaped as a child grows toward adulthood and learns the attitudes, values, beliefs, and behavior that form character.

It shouldn't be too surprising, then, to find that when a person is born again as a child of God, the

Lord chooses to put him in a new family. It shouldn't be too surprising that growth toward Christian maturity—again, the development of new attitudes, values, beliefs, and behavior as a distinctive Christian character is formed—should also be a family affair.

"Therefore, encourage one another and build each other up, just as in fact you are doing," Paul reminded the Thessalonians. "Live in peace with each other . . . warn those who are idle, encourage the timid, help the weak, be patient with everyone" (1 Thess. 5: 11, 13, 14). Just as the family is sensitive to each individual's needs, so there is to be sensitivity to each brother and sister in the church. In this context of family love, each can be encouraged and built up.

The Thessalonian letters help us see the quality of relationships appropriate to the family of God. As believers strive together to be responsive to the Word, they provide continual examples for each other (1 Thess. 1: 7; 2: 14). Within the family is an intense love, a love that reaches out and seeks to draw others close. "You yourselves have been taught by God to love each other. And in fact, you do love all the brothers," Paul praised the Thessalonians (1 Thess. 4: 9, 10). In the closeness of the family, we verbally exhort and instruct each other (1 Thess. 2: 11; 4: 1). In our concern for each other, we comfort and encourage (1 Thess. 4: 18; 5: 14). The love is so real, the belonging so sure, that we don't hesitate even to admonish or discipline (1 Thess. 5: 14; 2 Thess. 3: 6, 14).

*The church of God is intended to function as a family.* In the context of a growing relationship of mutual love, God the Holy Spirit works to transform.

*Lost life-style?* Perhaps more than any of the other factors, the loss of a family relationship in Christ's church can deaden and distort Christian life. In His last evening with the disciples, Jesus left them, and us, this commandment: "Love one another. As I have loved you, so you must love one another" (John 13:34). Christ was not making a "suggestion." His words express something so basic to the gospel message that they are cast in commandment form: "You must love one another." This is no optional call. Love for one another is utterly imperative. Family love is the key to transformation. And transformation is the first purpose of the church.

If we're frustrated by a lack of personal growth, one of the first places to look for an explanation is at our relationships with other Christians. Is our local church a family? Have we developed the intimate brother-sister relationship within our fellowship that marked the Thessalonian fellowship? Do we draw close, comfort, encourage, exhort, instruct, admonish, and even discipline one another? When the community of faith loses these family qualities, something basic to the gospel has been lost as well.

We can summarize several distinctives about the New Testament church as portrayed in Scripture that give us clues to Christianity's vitality:
- Truth, contextualized
- Love, exemplified
- Transformation, emphasized

BIBLE ALIVE SERIES

Vitality for us today involves the experience of these same dynamics that, in the gospel, are our heritage too.

## STUDYING THE NEW TESTAMENT

The **Bible Alive** books you're studying are designed for a simple purpose: to help you study the Scripture yourself. This text isn't a commentary, explaining Bible passages verse by verse. It's not a series of sermons based on Bible thoughts or chapters. Instead, it is a guide to personal Bible study. It's designed to orient you to a particular book or passage of Scripture and then to provide questions that will lead you to your own discoveries in the inspired text.

Several things are important as you move along:

*Historical context.* The writing of every book of Scripture is rooted in historical events and reflects the specific movements of God in that time. To understand a passage of Scripture, it's important to have some knowledge of the historical setting.

Several historical features have been important in looking at Acts 16—19 and the Thessalonian epistles. First, they reflect a particularly dynamic period in the life of the early church. They portray the early days of its expansion into Europe, an expansion so explosive that it precipitated great social changes (such as the economic threat to the trades in Ephesus) and riots as well. What was it about the church in those days that made its gospel presentation so successful?

The ultimate answer is "the power of God." But

how did God mediate His power? We've looked at these portions of Scripture in view of the distinctives of the days in which they were penned.

Second, we need to see the broader cultural context. What was the New Testament world like? What were the ways of thinking, the values and attitudes, of the Hellenistic world? When we understand these background factors, what we read in the New Testament takes on fresh meaning.

*Methods of approach.* There are many different ways or methods of Bible study. So far our study has used a *topical* approach. That is, we've picked a single theme or topic and read and reread assigned passages to see what each says about the chosen topic. We've read 1 Thessalonians twice, looking first for core truths (doctrines) and then looking for relationships. (Soon you'll be asked to read it again to search out yet another theme!)

As we move on into 1 Corinthians in the next chapters, we'll use a different method: *synthesis,* or tracing the author's argument. In our 2 Corinthians studies, we'll feature a third method of study, the *biographical.*

The goal in using different methods is partly to help you learn how to use each of them in your own Bible study. Through these books I hope you'll gain Bible study skills as well as a knowledge of the content of Scripture. But the method has also been chosen to fit the character of the passages themselves.

*Relevant principles.* A final concept that guides these studies is that the Word of God is a *living*

**BIBLE ALIVE SERIES**

Word. Through Scripture God speaks to us in our present situation as well as speaking to us about His workings in the past. Bible study means seeking out timeless truths—principles to help us understand God's workings in all of human life.

Whenever we read the Bible, we need to ask not only, "What does the Bible say?" but also, "What does the Bible say *to me today?*" When I understand the message of Scripture in terms of its own day, then I can hear more clearly God's message to me today.

Coming to know the Bible—a very basic goal in these **Bible Alive** studies—means gaining a mastery of both the content of Scripture and its message. "What does the Bible say?" and "What does it mean?" are twin concerns that shape the study questions at the end of each chapter. They will lead you to explore the text *and* to think about the application of what you find.

So don't be satisfied simply to read these chapters. Follow through and use the *Going Deeper* suggestions, which will lead you into a personal study of God's Word itself. Our heritage and the recovery of hope are both revealed in the living Word of our God.

**GOING DEEPER**

*to personalize*

1. Read through 1 and 2 Thessalonians again. This time put a box like this around verses and

phrases that seem to describe relationships within this young church.

From your discoveries, write a brief paper entitled "God's Ideal for the Local Church."

2. The author suggests that the gospel's power to transform is a factor (along with its *core truths* and *relationships*) that God used to penetrate the ancient world. Read through 1 and 2 Thessalonians another time. Make a list of *transformations the Christian can expect to undergo*. (What values will change? What attitudes? What feelings? What qualities of character? What else?)

3. Choose *two* things from the above list of transformations that seem particularly important to you. Why do you want your life to move in these directions?

4. Do you feel your own local church is the kind of transforming community that the author suggests Christ's church is intended to be? What evidence would you give to support your opinion?

5. What can *you* do with other Christians to build the kind of relationships God will use to accomplish transformation?

*to probe*

1. Look at a book on Bible-study methods. What can you find out about the topical method? When is it a good method to use? What are some of its limitations?

2. One prominent theme in the Thessalonian epistles is the Second Coming of Christ. Write a series of statements summarizing in your own words

BIBLE ALIVE SERIES

what Paul says in these letters about Jesus' return. Can you put the events in a time sequence? Why, or why not?

Look back over the context of each Second Coming teaching. Is anything of importance lost when you take these statements out of their biblical context? If so, what, and why?

# 5
*1 Corinthians 1-4*

# ONE FAMILY, INDIVISIBLE

NEAR THE END OF HIS THIRD missionary journey, Paul wrote a letter to a church in trouble. Some seven years before, he and his companions had founded it in Corinth. Even though the members of the believing community there were richly gifted, the transformation process seemed constantly blocked.

Paul kept in touch with the Corinthian fellowship as he did with all the churches. Finally, after the latest verbal report from the family of Chloe, and after a delegation arrived from Corinth asking for Paul's judgment on specific questions, this first letter to the Corinthians was written.

It is an important letter for us to read and to understand. It helps us realize that our struggle for real and vital faith may be a long one. And it helps us understand today how you and I can resolve problems that have continued to plague the church up to the present time.

Corinth was an important city and had been from ancient days. Situated on the isthmus bearing its name, Corinth controlled land and sea trade routes. In New Testament times it was not only an important commercial city but also the administrative center of the Province of Achaia. Gundry's description gives us an idea of the cosmopolitan character of Corinth:

> The athletic games at Corinth were second only to the Olympics. The outdoor theater accommodated twenty thousand people, the roofed theater three thousand. Temples, shrines, and altars dotted the city. A thousand sacred prostitutes made themselves available at the Temple of the Greek goddess Aphrodite. The south side of the marketplace was lined with taverns equipped with underground cisterns for cooling the drinks.[1]

Noted for its lax morals and scandalous life-style, Corinth was a completely pagan society—a society that created many difficulties for the believers who lived there.

Even though the Corinthian church was struggling, Paul began his letter with words of commendation and confidence. He addresses people who have been "sanctified in Christ Jesus and called to be holy, together with all those everywhere who call on the name of our Lord Jesus Christ." He assures them that Christ "will keep you strong to the end, so that you will be blameless in the day of our Lord Jesus Christ. God, who has called you into fellowship with his Son Jesus Christ our Lord, is faithful" (1 Cor. 1:2, 8, 9).

This is important for us to remember. No matter how much our own Christian experience may seem to involve struggle, no matter how slow our growth, it is God who has called us into fellowship with Himself. And God is faithful. He *will* work in our lives and keep us strong.

But once Paul expresses this attitude of support and confidence, he plunges immediately into an analysis of the Corinthians' problems.

## AN APPROACH

Like most of Paul's epistles, 1 Corinthians is well organized and closely reasoned. The overall structure is controlled by Paul's purpose. He introduces each new problem with a simple phrase: "Now concerning . . ." or simply "Now. . . ."

The problems faced by the church of Corinth sound like a catalog of problems faced by many churches today:
- Division in the church (1—4)
- Discipline in the fellowship (5, 6)
- Marriage and divorce (7)
- Doctrinal differences (8—10)
- The misuse of spiritual (charismatic) gifts (12—14)

In addition, this letter touches on the role of women, the place of the Lord's Supper, and the centrality of the Resurrection in Christian teaching.

Each section of 1 Corinthians takes up a separate

topic. Within each section, Paul's thoughts are carefully organized and his explanations tightly reasoned.

*Tracing the argument.* When we come to tightly reasoned passages of Scripture, the most appropriate Bible-study method is to trace the writer's line of argument. We must be careful not to take a verse out of its context and interpret it as though it stood by itself. A verse is fully understood only when we see how it fits with what precedes and what follows it.

How do we trace the argument? Here's an approach we can use with 1 Corinthians:

1. Read and reread the Bible section to determine its subject.
2. Make a one-sentence summary of each paragraph within the section.
3. Rework sentences into a brief paraphrase of the section.
4. Examine each paragraph of the text in detail.
5. Determine and apply major teachings (principles).

Working with the first four chapters of 1 Corinthians, let's see what can be discovered.

*1. Read and reread the Bible section to determine its subject.* Several things are quickly apparent. Paul talks a great deal about *wisdom.* This word and *wise* appear no fewer than twenty-seven times in the four-chapter section.

At the same time, it's clear that Paul isn't concerned with some intellectual debate about the relationship between faith and philosophy. He begins immediately in 1:10 to express his central concern: "I appeal to you . . . that there may be no divisions among you and that you may be perfectly united in mind and thought." The Corinthians have formed parties, or cliques, based on the supposed superiority of various Christian leaders. There was a "Paul party," an "Apollos party," a "Peter party," and some very spiritual types who claimed they were just the "Jesus party." These divisions destroyed the unity of the family and created dissension.

So we give the section a title:
*Maintaining Unity in the Church Family.*

Somehow, wisdom is critical here. As we trace the thought progression of the passage paragraph by paragraph, we see that grasping God's kind of wisdom is, in fact, the solution.

*2. Make a one-sentence summary of each paragraph within the section.* This is our next step: to say in one sentence the main thought or thrust of each paragraph.

Let's start with 1 Corinthians 1:10-12:

> I appeal to you, brothers, in the name of our Lord Jesus Christ, that all of you agree with one another so that there may be no divisions among you and that you may be perfectly united in mind and thought. My brothers, some from Chloe's household have informed me that there are quarrels among you. What I mean is this: One of you says, "I follow Paul"; another, "I follow Apollos"; another, "I follow Cephas"; still another, "I follow Christ."

What is the subject of this paragraph? What is the focus?

If we emphasize the problem, we might summarize this way:
*The division in your church fellowship is wrong.*

If we emphasize the goal, we'll pick up the subject from Paul's very first sentence: *I urge you to resolve your differences and restore unity in your church fellowship.*

Very often in translations of Paul's writings we'll find that the first sentence of a paragraph is a key to the subject. So let's choose the second summary (above) as the subject for this paragraph (although the first is not wrong). In developing summary sentences, there will always be room for different ways of stating the same thing.

Working through the entire passage, we may come up with summary sentences like the following:

| Paragraph | Verses | Summary Sentence |
|---|---|---|
| 1 | 1:10-12 | I urge you to resolve your differences and restore unity in your church fellowship. |
| 2 | 1:13-17 | The central fact is Christ, and that in Him we are one. |
| 3 | 1:18-25 | God's wisdom as shown in Christ is really at odds with man's "wise" approach to things. |
| 4 | 1:26-31 | In fact, it is Christ and not some superior wisdom who has brought you righteousness, holiness, and redemption! |
| 5 | 2:1-5 | I purposely kept my message simple when with you in order that your full reliance might be on the crucified Jesus. |
| 6 | 2:6-10 | Of course, there is a divine wisdom—but this |

|    |         |                                                                                                                                                                         |
|----|---------|-------------------------------------------------------------------------------------------------------------------------------------------------------------------------|
|    |         | comes through revelation, and its source is not in man's discoveries.                                                                                                   |
| 7  | 2:11-16 | This wisdom involves a person coming to grasp God's thoughts, something that demands both hearing the revealed words and being enlightened by the Holy Spirit.          |
| 8  | 3:1-4   | But you! Your jealousy and quarreling make it clear that you think and act on a merely human level.                                                                     |
| 9  | 3:5-9   | Who do you think is important—we servants, or the God who works through us?                                                                                             |
| 10 | 3:10-15 | I'm thankful for the privilege of serving, but my foundation is Jesus, and what I build will be evaluated one day.                                                      |
| 11 | 3:16-17 | But don't you realize that the true construction is going on in your lives, that *you* are God's sacred temple, and that we all must build (not tear down!) the growing structure? |
| 12 | 3:18-23 | So don't fool yourselves with all those childish arguments about which leader is better; abandon that kind of thing, and focus on all that God has given you in Christ. |
| 13 | 4:1-5   | Grasp this principle: God Himself is the source of all that a man possesses, so how can anyone boast about having "superior" gifts or skills?                           |
| 14 | 4:8-13  | Rather than trying to build our own little empires, we apostles have abandoned all, having chosen humiliation, weakness, hunger, and persecution as our lot.            |
| 15 | 4:14-16 | As your father, I warn you to imitate me in this and get your priorities back into harmony with reality.                                                                |

16   4:18-21   And I warn you: unity in the family is so vital that in God's power I will discipline you when I come unless you abandon your worldly arrogance!

*3. Rework sentences into a brief paraphrase of the section.* This involves going back over your sentence outline and seeing if the thought of each sentence is clearly connected to what precedes and what follows. Can you read them through together and follow the apostle's thinking clearly? Does the whole thing make sense?

The great value of this brief paraphrase is that it counteracts a common flaw in Bible study: we tend to lose sight of the whole. In a good summary paraphrase, the whole passage of Scripture is brought into clear view and is kept there—even when we go back to examine the content of a verse or paragraph more closely.

Here are the sentence summaries, reworked into a paragraph:

### UNITY IN THE CHURCH FAMILY
### 1 Corinthians 1—4

I urge you to resolve your differences and restore unity in the church family. Remember, Christ is the center of our life, and in Him we *are* one.

This may not sound like a very "wise" argument, but then the message of Christ and His cross has always been at odds with human wisdom. And Christ, not some super "wisdom," brought you your righteousness, holiness, and redemption. That's why I kept my message simple when I was with you, that you might rely only on the crucified Lord.

Of course there is a divine wisdom, but it comes by revelation and not human discovery. This wisdom involves learning to think God's thoughts, something that requires both hearing the revealed words and being enlightened by the Holy Spirit.

But you! Why, your jealousy and quarreling make it very clear that you think and act like mere men. Who do you think is important: we servants, or God who works through us? I'm thankful I can serve, but my foundation is Jesus, and one day what I build will be evaluated. (Don't you even grasp the fact that the true construction is going on *in your lives* and that *you* are God's sacred temple? Building up people, not tearing them down, is doing God's work!)

So don't deceive yourselves with all those childish arguments over leaders. Abandon that foolish game and focus again on all that is yours in Jesus, you who are not on trial before any human jury! Can't you grasp the basic principle? God Himself is the source of all. How then can we boast about anyone's superior gifts or skills?

Why, rather than trying to build our own little kingdoms, we apostles have abandoned all that and have chosen humiliation, weakness, hunger, and even persecution as our lot. So I warn you. Imitate me in this, and get your priorities back in order. And this is a warning. Unity in the family is so vital that, in God's own power I will discipline you when I come unless you abandon your worldly arrogance!

What a powerful passage! And what a vital message for a divided Church today.

**4. *Examine each paragraph of the text in detail.*** At this point, with the overview of the argument in mind, we want to go back and look into each paragraph more closely. It is *now* that a verse-by-verse approach to Bible study can be helpful, for now our understanding of the thoughts and phrases expressed will be guided by an understanding of the context.

Often at this point we'll make exciting discoveries and see fresh meaning in verses that have become so familiar we once read over them without thought. Often, too, we'll make a discovery that will lead us to go back to our paraphrase and make a change, bringing the whole thrust of the passage into clearer focus. A study of the details of the text is always more fruitful when we have first gained a grasp of the argument of the larger unit.

As a matter of fact, this very point is one that Paul makes for us in 1 Corinthians 1 and 2. He has pointed out that man's way of thinking (human "wisdom") and God's way of thinking (His "foolishness") really do *not* correspond. The cross is given as an example of this fact. Who would have ever imagined that God would give us righteousness, holiness, and redemption by means of the criminal execution of His own Son!

To the Greek mind the whole notion was idiotic; salvation, if there were such a thing, would have to come through some appeal to man's capacity to achieve. Furthermore, the Greek mind viewed God as immutable and immortal, hence the gospel presentation of incarnation, the cross, and resurrection were simply ruled out; the gospel contradicted one of the axioms of classical Greek philosophy.

To the Hebrew, the whole thing was foreign as well. Deliverance would come in another Exodus, with God breaking into history to perform miracles and punish Israel's enemies. A suffering Savior? Never! Israel would settle for nothing less than a conquering King.

While the Greek and the Jew each clung to his own notion of how God must act, God had His own ideas. The cross meant that each must surrender his own way of thinking and submit to a divine wisdom that operates on principles *basically* different from those that appeal to human thought.

Man is impressed by human accomplishment; God chose to use the despised things.

Man is impressed by strength; God chose to use weakness.

Even in the church, the human tendency is to seek to build little kingdoms around differences—different leaders, different doctrines, different ways of baptizing, different likes and dislikes in music. Paul tells us it is *God's* way to reject all that and to build *unity* around the one thing all Christians have in common: Jesus.

Paul's whole argument here is a warning to the church at Corinth—and to us—that we must learn to look at issues from the divine viewpoint. We must realize God doesn't think the same way we do. We must be willing to surrender our own way of thinking and earnestly search out His.

How? Paul tells us. God has revealed His thoughts in "words taught by the Spirit" (1 Cor. 2:13). And

God has given believers the Holy Spirit to interpret the written Word (2:9-15). In the Word and the Spirit, Paul tells us, we have been given an astounding gift: "We have the mind of Christ" (2:16). Searching the Word, guided by the Holy Spirit, we are to learn God's wisdom and gradually grow to evaluate all things from His unique perspective.

This is why a tracing-the-argument approach to Bible study is so important. We're prone to grasp a single verse or teaching and try to make it fit our way of thinking. We're apt to use the Bible to try to prove our point of view or disprove someone else's. Instead, we are called to study the Scripture to help us *abandon* our point of view and submit ourselves instead to God's. In disciplining ourselves to trace the argument of a section of Scripture, we guard against our natural tendency to misuse, and we set ourselves to grasp the very thoughts of God.

*5. Determine and apply major teachings (principles).* It is fascinating to see how Paul went back to basic principles in dealing with the problem of division in the Corinthian church. What is wrong with division?

*Christ is one.* Unity in the family is vital because we model this reality through unity.

*Christ is the source.* Any gift a servant of the Lord may have is just that, a gift he has received. There is no room for pride either *for* him or *in* him. If God blesses you through one of His servants, address your praise and build your loyalty toward *Him.*

Paul calls the Corinthians and us to test our attitudes and evaluate our own actions. The Church's one foundation *is* Jesus Christ, her Lord. Reaffirming that foundation, the Corinthian church could again find the family unity that had been lost.

And so can we.

## GOING DEEPER

*to personalize*

Most of this chapter is given to describing a method of Bible study you'll use *before* reading the next chapters of this book. Thus many of the suggested assignments focus on the next section of 1 Corinthians. But before going on to them, do the following projects guided by the sentence outline and paraphrase summary to master the content and message of these first four chapters.

1. Look at all twenty-seven occurrences of *wise* or *wisdom* in the text. From this passage, how would you define these terms? What do you think Paul's concept of wisdom means for believers today?

2. Read 1 Corinthians 1:10—4:21. *Keep clearly in mind how each paragraph fits into the argument of the whole.* Mark any verses that seem to you to be more meaningful or more clear when seen in this context. Note also how a particular verse or thought might be *misunderstood* if the context were not clear.

3. On page 72 the author noted two principles that Paul presents as keys to his argument (Christ is one, and Christ is the source). See if you can discover additional basic principles that seem to underlie the apostle's points.

4. Make a list of *specific situations* in your local church and in the Church at large in which the

teachings of 1 Corinthians 1—4 need to be applied. Then choose *one* situation from your list and write a letter to those involved, seeking to help grasp the principles that could bring unity and harmony. (You may or may not be led to send the letter.)

*in preparation*

*Before* reading the next chapter in this text, use the method of Bible-study outline on page 64. Carefully trace the argument of 1 Corinthians 5—6. Be sure to *write* what you do in each of these steps.

1. Robert H. Gundry, *A Survey of the New Testament* (Grand Rapids: Zondervan, 1970), pp. 275-76.

# 6
*1 Corinthians 5–6*

# THE DUTY TO DISCIPLINE

I'VE JUST TALKED LONG-DISTANCE to the pastor of the church where I serve as an elder. One of the women in the local family, who for a time was growing rapidly in the faith, has recently gone through a painful divorce. At one point she had had an affair with a neighbor, a situation about which we had confronted her and had been assured that it was over.

Just two days ago we discovered she is now living with her paramour. And, as members of the family of God, we are now responsible to discipline her.

It's not an easy prospect.

We naturally draw back from this kind of confrontation. In the family, our deepest desire is to support and love, so discipline seems harsh and unloving. Can we really *care* and at the same time deal freely with sin in the fellowship, even passing judgment on it and the sinner as Paul does in 1 Corinthians 5? How, after Paul has warned us against judging him and his fellow leaders (4:1-5), dare we judge a fellow believer? Paul reported that he was not even competent to judge himself (4:4)!

Yet, in a society such as first-century Corinth, there was a sure need for discipline. Immorality was an accepted part of the Corinthian life-style. These patterns of thought, these old passions and desires, were sure to appear again and again. An individualism and relativism much like that of our own day stressed "freedom" and insisted that even though something may not be right for you, it might be right for me. Today's typical approach to pornography, seeking to change the nature of the filthy by labeling it "mature," fits the culture of Corinth. The sophisticated people of Corinth were as adept as the sophisticated people of today in pretending that evil is good and good evil.

In a world like theirs and ours, in which the "rights" of the individual are stressed while old distinctions between right and wrong are blurred, there are sure to be times when immorality and other kinds of sin infect even the Church of God. The old ways of thinking die hard. Transformation, while real, is a gradual and progressive process of change. On the journey to Christian maturity, both individuals and a local church family can falter.

That's what has happened in my own local congregation just now. And that's what happened in the Corinthian church. Facing the issue head-on, Paul helps them—and us—think through a number of difficult questions. In the process, Paul helps us discover more of God's mind and heart.

## PAUL'S INSTRUCTION

This Corinthian passage, which you've studied already (see *Going Deeper, in preparation,* p. 74), deals directly and decisively with the issue of discipline. Your paraphrase summary, which may look something like this, highlights the central issues:

### DISCIPLINE IS ESSENTIAL
### 1 Corinthians 5—6

Deal decisively with that case of sexual immorality you've been tolerating—put the man out of your fellowship! How can you have been proud of your toleration? Don't you realize such old taints can spoil the new person you are in Christ? Earlier, I told you not to associate with the sexually immoral, and I meant specifically those who call themselves brothers. I don't judge non-Christians; it's those within who are to be judged—and in this case expelled.

Even things such as lawsuits and disputes are to be settled within the family. Why, the continued existence of such things is a tragic spiritual defeat. People practicing sin have no place in God's Kingdom; you *were* like that, some of you, but after being washed and sanctified and justified in Jesus, all that is to be put behind. Don't misuse the "Everything is permissible" principle. That is subordinate to the fact that Jesus is Lord. You can never take that body of yours, a member of Christ, and unite it with some prostitute! Utterly reject sexual immorality, for, as the temple of God's Holy Spirit, you belong to Him now.

At first glance this summary does not seem to help us answer the difficult questions, such as: How dare we judge others? Why must we discipline within the family? Doesn't discipline violate others' freedom? How do we discipline? What kinds of things are valid issues for discipline?

Yet, going back over the passage and remembering the larger context established in the first four chapters of this book, we can find important answers.

Before you read on, you may want to stop and go back over the passage, looking for your own answers. If you do, record your thoughts on the following chart:

---

**INSIGHTS INTO DISCIPLINE**

1. How dare we judge others?

2. What kinds of things are valid causes for discipline?

3. Why must we discipline within the family?

4. How do we discipline?

5. Doesn't discipline violate others' rights?

---

With your observations recorded, let's think about these questions together:

*How dare we judge others?* The answer to the first

question is clear. God tells us that we must (5: 4, 5, 9; 6: 2-4). At first this seems strange, especially as Paul has earlier told us that the relative value of any Christian leader's ministry is not to be hauled before any human jury. But it soon becomes clear that different things are being judged here. In the first case, the Corinthians were choosing up sides and rallying around their favorite preachers. This is hardly the kind of judgment Paul is calling for in chapters 5 and 6.

Some things we have no right to judge. Other things we must judge.

This really should be an obvious principle. I'm not a nuclear physicist, so I wouldn't be called in to judge the safety or danger of a new atomic power plant. But, as an educator, I'm often invited to schools to evaluate and judge curriculums or programs. In areas where I am not competent to judge, I must refrain; in the other areas I should speak up.

In the church some questions—such as another's motives or his service for God—are definitely not in my province. But God *has* made us responsible for some questions in the church. And in those areas we must accept our responsibility and judge.

*What kinds of things are valid issues for discipline?* As we look at the Corinthians passage, it becomes even more clear: *Things God has already defined as sin! We* are not saying, "Sexual immorality is sin." God has already made that determination. In acting to judge the immoral brother, the church family was only choosing to side with God's judgment that already had been pronounced.

It's striking that the other things Paul mentions are those also clearly specified in Scripture as sins: idolatry, adultery, homosexuality, thievery, drunkenness. God has already pronounced judgment on all of them. In these areas the church also must speak out with God's voice. Our judgment must agree with His.

But just a minute. Doesn't the text speak of "idolaters" rather than idolatry? Of "homosexual offenders" rather than homosexuality? Yes, and this wording is extremely significant—not because it indicates a person rather than a sin, but because it indicates *a person who is habitually practicing the sin.* Paul is not saying that an individual is to be expelled from the fellowship for a single act or failure. After all, transformation is not instantaneous; we need to give each other room to grow. But when a person habitually practices sexual immorality or thievery or homosexuality, then the family is to accept the responsibility of discipline and to act.

Even the "lawsuits" and "dispute" of chapter 6 (vv. 1, 7) fall into the realm of practice. God has already judged; the first four chapters of this very letter underline the fact that factions and quarreling within the Body of Christ are completely out of harmony with God's will for the church. As the family of God, the church is to reflect in its unity the great reality that in Christ we *are* one.

What church discipline involves, then, is judgment (1) of a practice God's Word has clearly condemned (2) when that sin is habitually practiced (3) by one who claims to be in the family of God.

*Why must we discipline within the family?* One answer is given in this passage. The family of God is to reflect His own purity. Permitting sin in Christ's body will taint the whole, and spread (5: 6-8).

This point is particularly significant when we remember that the church is God's chosen agency for transformation. Within the fellowship of the family we find our examples, our support, our encouragement, our instruction, our admonition—all those influences God uses to help us enter into the great realities we're called to experience in Christ. A church family torn by disputes or soiled by the presence of those committed to habitual sins loses its power to transform. For the church to fulfill God's purpose, discipline is a necessity.

There's one other point, made not here but in 2 Corinthians, that we need to remember. Discipline is also the *loving* way to deal with the sinner. The goal is not to cut him off but to work for his restoration by helping him to sense the seriousness of sin and to respond to God's call to holiness. When the Corinthian church obeyed Paul's demand, the result was the restoration of the sexually immoral brother (2 Cor. 2: 5-11).

*How do we discipline?* In one case, discipline simply demanded choosing a fellow believer to act as an arbitrator and settle the lawsuit that was dividing two brothers (6: 3-5). In the case of the continuing immorality, we know that Paul had given instruction about such cases when he was with them, and in an earlier (lost) letter (5: 9-11). We can assume that his instruction included an explanation of the process

Jesus outlines in Matthew 18:15-17. Only when the sinner fails to respond to the loving admonition first of individuals and then of the whole leadership of the local church is the final step to be taken. But that final step *is* to be taken with the person who will not respond. He is to be cut off from the fellowship of the family until he repents. In Jesus' words, "Treat him as you would a pagan or a tax collector." In Paul's restatement, which captures the meaning of those words exactly, "With such a man do not even eat" (1 Cor. 5:9).

*Doesn't discipline violate others' rights?* This question reflects an individualism characteristic of both Hellenistic times and our own. Then, as now, people claimed personal freedom and privilege, insisting, "Everything is permissible for men" (6:12).

But we Christians are no longer independent, and our "rights" are no longer paramount. For one thing, we now belong to the Lord. Our bodies, as well as our hearts and minds, are His. *He holds the right to be Lord of this body of ours.*

As a result, while free from all external bondage, we exercise our freedom within the limits imposed by God's purpose for our lives. "You were bought at a price," Paul reminds the Corinthians. "Therefore honor God with your body" (6:20).

When it comes to discipline in the church of Christ, we do not hesitate to act because of concern that we might violate our brother's rights. Instead, we are willing to act because God has charged us to uphold *His rights.*

And, of course, we act in discipline because of love

for our brother. He will only find the meaning of his life, and we ours, in full fellowship with our Lord. In discipline the family invites a brother to return to Him.

## GOING DEEPER

*to personalize*

1. What *principles* (the fifth step in our tracing-the-argument study approach) did you find in this passage? List them, and, for each one, give at least *three* illustrations of how it might be applied today.

2. Do local churches discipline today? Give evidence for your opinion.

3. What factors are involved in making discipline *effective?* (For instance, the church, as we've seen it in the New Testament, is a family. Being cut off from the family and its intimate relationships can really hurt. If there is no family kind of relationship between members, would expulsion mean anything?)

4. Using the concepts presented on pages 79 and 80, make a list of ten items that you believe *are* matters for discipline. Then make a list of ten items that you believe are *not* matters for discipline.

What seem to be the most significant differences between the two lists?

5. Study Matthew 18:15-17. If the elders in the author's church follow this procedure in dealing with the situation described at the beginning of this chapter, what will they do?

6. One other passage of Scripture is very important on this topic of discipline: Hebrews 12:5-15.

Study it carefully. Then make a list of statements that you believe express the main points to be kept in mind when approaching church discipline.

7. Finally, read through 1 Corinthians 7. We'll come back to this chapter later.

*in preparation*

Because we're using a method designed to trace the argument in larger sections of Scripture, we'll skip 1 Corinthians 7 temporarily and move on to chapters 8—10. Before reading on in the next chapter of this text, use our basic method again to entitle chapters 8—10, to give sentence outlines of each paragraph, and then to build them into a short paraphrase. Finally, locate and state basic principles found in the passage.

This should be a fascinating study. It raises this very contemporary question: Is doctrine a valid issue over which to divide the church?

# 7

*1 Corinthians 8–10*

# THE RIGHT TO BE WRONG

IT SEEMS PECULIAR. In a faith that claims to possess truth, Paul insisted on protecting the right of brothers to be wrong!

This is actually what we discover in this powerful section of 1 Corinthians. Among the issues raised by the Corinthians and carried to Paul by Stephanas, Fortunatus, and Achaicus (16:17) was a doctrinal dispute. The church appealed to Paul to settle the dispute, to tell them which side was right. Paul settled it by explaining how Christian practice is to be guided. He was careful not to give either side a club with which to bludgeon the other. Something else was involved in their doctrinal conflict that takes priority, something more important than being "right." When we grasp the spirit of Paul's teaching here, we will have a very necessary guide for us today.

We've seen that the New Testament church broke into the Hellenistic world with a gospel of revolutionary truth *and* with a revolutionary relationship: love. The impact of the church was related to both truth and love, and to the fulfilled promise of transformation. We can expect to have an equal impact on the twentieth-century world as the core truth is communicated, contextualized for our culture; as the message of God's love is communicated, demonstrated in the Christian's love relationships; and as the power of God is communicated, proven in the believer's transformation.

But what happens when there is disagreement in Christ's Body over truth? What happens when we are forced by our consciences to disagree, not over favorite leaders (1 Cor. 1—4), but over truth itself? How can we preserve love in a dispute?

Sometimes the answer has been given: "Contend for the truth. Break away from those who are not doctrinally 'pure.' " At other times this answer has been given: "Doctrine is unimportant! Emphasize love, and let go of truth for the sake of fellowship."

*Either of these solutions short-circuits the dynamic of the Body of Christ.* In New Testament times and our own, it is the *harmonious* testimony of truth, love, and transformation that has provided compelling evidence of the reality of Christ and overwhelmed the defenses of pagan cultures.

Our solution to the problem of doctrinal differences has to affirm both truth and love. That kind of solution is just what Paul offers in 1 Corinthians 8—10.

## CULTURAL BACKGROUND

Before summarizing the thrust of this section, it will be helpful to point out the situation in Corinth and to note that Paul is dealing with *two* problems in this question about "meat sacrificed to idols" (8:1).

Leon Morris helps us understand why this question was a difficult one for believers in the first century.

> First, it was an accepted social practice to have meals in a temple, or in some place associated with an idol. "It was all part and parcel of the formal etiquette in society" (Moffatt). The kind of occasion, public or private, when people were likely to come together socially was the kind of occasion when a sacrifice was appropriate. To have nothing to do with such gatherings was to cut oneself off from most social intercourse with one's fellows . . . . Secondly, most of the meat sold in the shops had first been offered in sacrifice. Part of the victim was always offered on an altar to the god, part went to the priests, and usually part to the worshippers. The priests customarily sold what they could not use. It would be very difficult to know for sure whether meat in a given shop had been part of a sacrifice or not. Notice that there are two separate questions: taking part in idol feasts, and the eating of meat bought in the shops, but previously part of a sacrifice.[1]

What should the Corinthians do? Not go to dinner at friends' homes because the food served would have been offered previously to pagan gods or goddesses? (Actually Paul had taught them in 5:9-12 that they were *not* to cut themselves off from pagan people—even from idolators.) As for their own homes, the temple meat markets were the normal places to shop. Should a Christian become a vegetarian?

In struggling with this issue, the Corinthians rightly went back to core truths; they searched the realities revealed by God (we call them "doctrines") for guidelines. But they kept coming up with different answers! It was this doctrinal dispute—not just a "practical issue"—that led them to appeal to the apostle, asking him for guidance in understanding how the truth should be applied.

Many commentators feel that Paul, in answering, actually quoted from their letter to him. These phrases seem most likely to represent the different doctrinal views that divided the Corinthians:

- "An idol is nothing at all in the world" (8:4).
- "Food does not bring us near to God; we are no worse if we do not eat, and no better if we do" (8:8).

These clearly reflect the arguments of those who found no difficulty in fitting into their culture's patterns. In fact, their freedom to do so was a joyful realization of great doctrinal truths. God is *one*. All the gods and goddesses they had tried to appease and had worshiped in the unlikely expectation of some kind of aid didn't even exist! Freed from the emptiness of that whole system, they laughed at the lumps of stone and metal that once had held them in bondage. As for food, they also realized the irrelevance of all the rituals through which they had once sought to please God. Relationship with God in

Christ is a living thing, a vital, personal transaction. What we eat or don't eat doesn't delight Him. It's what's in our hearts, not in our stomachs, that is Jesus' concern (Matt. 15:17-20).

Paul gently agreed with the insights of this party and then proceeded to show them how it's possible to be "right" and still be wrong! In being right, they hadn't yet grasped the whole truth.

## TRACING THE ARGUMENT

It's difficult to summarize paragraphs so packed with ideas as some are in this section of Corinthians. But your summary may read something like this:

### THE RIGHT TO BE WRONG
### 1 Corinthians 8—10

Let's begin thinking about this idol question in terms of *love* rather than *knowledge*. Beginning from knowledge, we do conclude that idols are nothing. But this isn't the customary view. Someone might be led by your example at an idol feast to eat against his conscience. If you thus damage a brother for whom Christ died, *that* is a sin against the Lord Himself.

Look, you know I'm an apostle. As such, I, too, might claim certain rights, such as the right to be supported by you. But I gave up this right, and I work to earn my living. I freely surrender my rights and choose to live as a slave to everyone in order to reach them. It's like an athlete. He gives up many things while in training in order to win the prize. Well, my prize is people.

Now, as to your "knowledge," don't be ignorant of the fact that Israel's experience speaks to us Christians. Idolatry led Israel into all sorts of immorality, and brought on God's judgment. Are you to feel secure in your knowledge of the emptiness of idolatry? Watch out that you don't fall into the common temptations associated with it!

Really, flee idolatry. Our communion is with Christ, and our identity with those who are one in Him. While idols are nothing, pagan sacrifices are offered to very real demons who are behind the pagan systems. So *don't* participate in idol feasts. Don't insist on your rights and your freedom! Choose what's beneficial to you and others.

But don't make a big issue of meat purchased at temple meat markets. If someone else makes an issue of it—like saying, "This is temple meat!"—then don't eat it, for his sake. God *doesn't* care what's in your stomach, but even eating and drinking can be done to God's glory. In this case, that means considering the impact of your actions on others—Jews, Greeks, and your brothers—and being guided in what you do by concern for their own good rather than the rightness of your position. This is what I do as I follow Jesus, so follow my example.

We need to grasp several critical points in the Corinthian passage if we're to see the progression of Paul's argument here.

*Limitations on knowledge (1 Cor. 8:1-3).* Paul is responding here to the stance taken by the Corinthians. Each side had based its whole position on the question of "Who's right?" Each based its conviction that it was right on an appeal to superior knowledge. Paul warns that approaching *any* issue in the family solely from the point of view of what we "know" is inadequate and dangerous. Why? Because each side in the argument has at least some grasp of truth ("We all possess knowledge," v. 1a). But putting the emphasis completely on truth tends to create pride ("Knowledge puffs up," v. 1b). Actually, our grasp of truth is incomplete; our insistence on our truth as the whole truth is extremely dangerous ("The man who thinks he knows something does not yet know as he ought to know," v. 2).

Immediately, then, Paul establishes the fact that in their dispute the Corinthians have approached the issue in the wrong way. They have forgotten love. They have forgotten the imperfection of their understanding of God's truth and have, in effect, cut themselves off from growth in understanding through their pride in knowing more than their brothers.

How do we approach disagreements over doctrine? Paul says to be sure to *begin* with *love*. Why? First, because love is the key to transformation. In the loving family of God, the Spirit works to transform attitudes, values, behavior, understanding—the total personality. What Paul is saying is that *where there is love in the body, there will be openness to God.* As we open our life to God, He guides us into "the knowledge of the truth" (Heb. 10:26).

We can diagram this key concept in this way:

### Dispute Handled by Knowledge

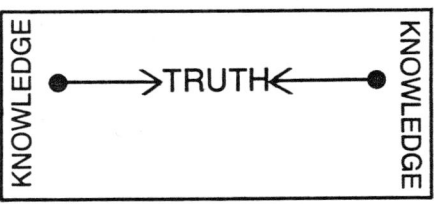

In the confrontation approach, each side claims to know more truth than the other. This leads to pride and the encouragement of a closed mind to aspects of truth not yet grasped. It does not help either side open up to God the Spirit to be taught by Him.

### Dispute Handled Through Love

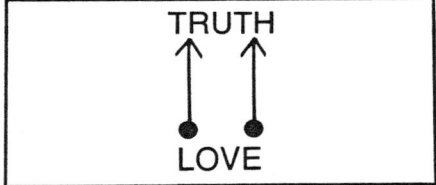

In the commitment approach, each side affirms its love for and acceptance of the other. Side by side, without false pride, each humbly admits the limitations of its knowledge and concentrates on helping the other love God better. This leads to both sides being open to God and the teaching ministry of the Spirit.

When differences are approached in love, there is no retreat from commitment to truth. Instead, there is a desire to discover the truth and grasp it better—together.

*Paul's rights (1 Cor. 9)*. At first it's a temptation to think that chapter 9 is unrelated to chapter 8. How did Paul move from talking about meat offered to idols to the subject of apostolic rights?

He was pointing out a factor the Corinthians had overlooked, an issue that was vitally important in their essentially doctrinal dispute. The attitude of those who knew an idol had no real existence was this: "I've got the truth, and therefore I have a *right* to eat meat offered to idols." Doctrinal correctness *in itself* seemed enough.

Paul, however, confronted them with something they hadn't thought of. Even if they were right about idols and were perfectly free to eat the meat at idol feasts with a clear conscience, was their *insistence on exercising their rights* truly a Christian approach? Which has priority—our rights, or our brother's well-being? What do we care about most—ourselves, or children in God's family who may not have grown in our "strong" maturity yet?

In chapter 8 Paul concluded that the Corinthians, rather than taking pride in their knowledge of the truth, really ought to have been ashamed of their attitude of unconcern for others. Chapter 9 is a personal example; Paul wasn't just "preaching at" the Corinthians. He had chosen to give up his rights and privileges as an apostle *for their sake.*

*More truth (1 Cor. 10)*. Chapter 10 grows out of Paul's initial warning that the knowledge of truth is often incomplete. He had commended the Corinthians who knew that an idol was "nothing at all in the world" (8:4). But in chapter 10 he points out the dangers of idolatry. As far as participating in idol feasts is concerned, such things have always been associated with immorality (as they were in Corinth). Does a person identified with Jesus think it's right, by participating, to identify himself with all that culture associates with idol feasts? In idolatry are temptations common to all men; Christians aren't exempt (10:13)! While the idols are "nothing at all in the world," idolatry has always been used by demonic powers, which *are* real. Can a Christian, who shares in Communion and drinks "the cup of the Lord," go to an idolatrous feast and "drink . . . the cup of demons too" (v. 21)?

So their claim to "know" really was foolish. They were basing a justification of their actions on only part of the truth. Looking at the issue in a broader perspective, it's clear that their conclusion about participation in idol feasts was wrong.

Finally Paul pointed out that eating meat in a private home, even though it may have been purchased at a temple meat market, wasn't the same thing as participating in a festive and idolatrous party dedicated to some pagan god or goddess. If the host made an issue of the meat as having been offered to an idol, then, for the sake of *his* conscience, they were to refrain from eating. But otherwise, they were not to make an issue of it. Just remember, Paul says, that while the food itself is morally neutral, in eating or in drinking or in whatever we do, we can and are to seek God's glory and to be sensitive to what will lead to the salvation of the lost and the benefit of our brothers.

## ANALYSIS

There are several vital lessons for us in Paul's handling of this early doctrinal dispute.
- *Start from a commitment to love.* Even if a brother is wrong, we are not released from our obligation to love him.
- *Maintain a concern for truth.* Paul kept a balance. He kept on loving both sides in this issue, but he did not hesitate to make truth clear even when it revealed one position as wrong.
- *Be sensitive to the relational implications of truth.* One side in Corinth was so sure of being right—and sure that orthodoxy gave them the right to participate in idol feasts—that they disregarded *other* truths that focused on relationships in the family.
- *Don't treat one truth as the whole truth.* We need to look beyond the doctrine being disputed in order to be aware of other related truths of Scripture. By building their whole argument on the fact that idols are nothing, and overlooking the reality of demons and the immoral cultural associations of idolatrous celebrations, the "I can eat" party reached a wrong conclusion.

Keeping these principles in mind can help us when we have honest differences within our churches today.

*Paul's pattern.* The way Paul dealt with the error here was beautifully sensitive and loving. He even found it possible to commend those who were wrong for grasping the truth they had apprehended! He also commended them for their "strong" consciences. How wonderful that these men and women were able to cast off the attitude of a lifetime and, on the basis of God's Word as they understood it, find freedom from idolatrous bondage and fear. Anyone who is aware of the difficulties of pagan peoples held in such bondage (and modern missionary experiences testify over and over again to the reality of that bondage) would have to commend these Corinthians.

So rather than beginning by saying, "You're wrong!" Paul started by commending and affirming them.

In the rest of the discussion Paul kept the focus on the relational and encouraged the Corinthians to act for the benefit of their brothers. He let them know he expected as much, that he really believed they cared. Paul did point out straightforwardly that because of two factors (two truths) they had overlooked their position *was* wrong. But at the same time, he kept his appeal focused on *both* truth and love.

*Paul's promise.* How did Paul find the freedom himself to deal with error so gently and lovingly? How was he able to commend those who were wrong and to actually affirm their right to *be* wrong?

Paul operated on a vital premise—one we need to grasp. *Paul expected the Corinthians to grow.* He did not insist that everyone be doctrinally correct *now*. He knew that in the loving context of a family, which finds even the erring brother worthy of affirmation and concern, spiritual and personal growth *would* be taking place. As life was opened up to the Spirit of

God, He—the Teacher—would lead these brothers into all truth.

You and I can accept even doctrinal differences in the fellowship of the local church when we share this conviction. Our brothers—and we, too—are young. We have a long way to grow. At best, our understanding is incomplete. But God will bring us, through our love for one another and His transforming power, to the place where we *both* will have a more complete knowledge of God's truth.

## GOING DEEPER

*to personalize*

1. Imagine that you are a board member in a noncharismatic church and that several in the fellowship have had a tongues experience, which they are attempting to share with the others. A dispute quickly develops within the church family.

— How might this dispute be handled if approached on the basis of knowledge?

— How might it be handled if approached on the basis of love?

— What truths would you want to consider in addition to the truth about spiritual gifts?

— What would you expect to be the outcome in your local fellowship? How long do you think it would take for this to develop?

2. As the administrator of a Christian college, would you invite a person with a seriously different doctrinal position to teach in your school? Why, or why not?

BIBLE ALIVE SERIES

How is this situation *similar to* or *different from* the local-church situation with which Paul dealt?)

*in preparation*
First Corinthians 12—14 does deal with a situation similar to number 1 above. Using the method of tracing the argument, find out how Paul dealt with the whole area of spiritual gifts and their exercise.

1. Leon Morris, *The First Epistle of Paul to the Corinthians,* Tyndale New Testament Commentary, (Grand Rapids: Eerdmans, 1958), p. 168.

# 8
*1 Corinthians 12–14*

# TROUBLE OVER TONGUES

BY NOW IT SHOULD BE CLEAR. The New Testament church was not utopia!

Sometimes we tend to imagine it that way. Plagued by problems in a local congregation, we long for those early days again. We feel that somehow the church has lost its power, and we wonder how to recapture those supposed days of constant victory.

The New Testament church *was* dynamic.

Truth, love, and transformation were its distinctive characteristics in a world empty of each. But the same trio is meant to characterize the family of God in any age, including our own. The way to victory is always marked by struggle, growth, and time. Maturity comes gradually.

So let's not be discouraged if at times our churches

are troubled by differences, problems, and disputes. Let's remember that Paul wrote these letters when the church was vital and alive, and that even a vital, alive church has problems. It is not the absence of problems but *how we deal with them* that determines our continued growth toward the full experience of blessing.

In his letters, Paul is guiding us as well as the Corinthians to just this understanding. He wants us to know how to deal with issues likely to trouble any local church . . . including problems that may be caused by tongues.

## BACKGROUND

Once again, some insight into the first-century world is helpful as we approach what seems a very contemporary problem.

*Tongues.* In the New Testament we first meet tongues in Acts 2, when on the Day of Pentecost the Holy Spirit welded the disciples into a new body, the Church. Not only were there miraculous signs of fire and wind, but, filled with the Holy Spirit, the disciples began to "speak in other tongues as the Spirit enabled them" (v. 4).

"How is it," the observers acted in amazement, "that each of us hears them in his own native language?" (Acts 2:8).

Later, when we meet tongues in Acts, they again seem to be foreign languages (see Acts 10:44-46; 11:17).

Coming to 1 Corinthians, we learn that the

tongues-speaker himself did not understand what he was saying unless the gift of interpretation functioned as well. In fact, interpretation of tongues is specified here as a separate gift—a gift often possessed by a fellow believer. Tongues, then, was not used evangelistically in the early church but instead was exercised within the family, and then only when an interpreter was present to make the message intelligible to others (1 Cor. 14: 28).

Nothing in this passage rules out tongues as a valid expression of the Holy Spirit ministering through one of God's children. Instead, Paul sought to help the family put this rather spectacular gift in perspective.

*Cultural context.* It was universally accepted in the Hellenistic world that some persons were especially close to the gods. Usually the closeness was supposed to be manifested by trances, ecstatic speech, and other unusual or bizarre forms of behavior, which were taken to be evidence of special spiritual endowments. A person with epilepsy was said to have the "divine disease." The oracles at religious centers were often given drugs to provoke their utterances. The oracle at Delphi, so prominent in the early days of Greece, breathed volcanic fumes from a cleft in the rock of the temple floor, and her unconscious mutterings were then interpreted by priests.

It's not surprising that in Corinth those who spoke in tongues were felt to be especially spiritual.

This assumption led to problems in the Corinthian church, and Paul immediately began to deal with them. His very first words were: "Now about spiritual gifts, brothers, I do not want you to be ignorant" (12:1).

The word *gifts* should be placed in parentheses here, because it is not necessarily implied by the Greek word *pneumatikon*. As the alternate reading in the Revised Standard Version suggests, it might well be rendered "spiritual *persons.*" This probably better reflects the issue that troubled the Corinthians. These people were pagans just a short time ago, "somehow or other ... influenced and led astray to dumb idols" (12:2). It was dangerous for them to carry over into the Christian faith old notions about spirituality! Apparently they had been so influenced by the old assumptions that when someone in an ecstatic trance had pronounced an *anathema* ("be accursed") against Jesus Himself, some of the Corinthians had actually been swayed! They had taken the state of the person making the utterance as evidence of divine inspiration.

Paul says firmly that no one can say, "Jesus be cursed," by the Spirit of God. Neither would anyone caught up in such an experience (as were the oracles of pagan faiths) ever announce, "Jesus is Lord," unless indwelt by the Holy Spirit.

There was then (as now) a great danger that in their ignorance some in the church would be led away from true spirituality by an unwarranted emphasis on this more spectacular manifestation. Paul's response was not to attack tongues but rather to give a lengthy explanation of the Spirit's working in our lives. He touched on the function of spiritual gifts and on the nature of true spirituality.

## TRACING THE ARGUMENT

Our insight into backgrounds helps us entitle this important section of Corinthians and also helps us follow the apostle's train of thought. Compare your summary paraphrase of this passage with the following:

### TRUE SPIRITUALITY
### 1 Corinthians 12—14

Brothers, don't view spirituality from your old pagan perspective. God is at work in all of us, but the Spirit's work is manifested in different ways. Yet, it *is* the Spirit who shows Himself behind each gift, and these expressions of His presence are dedicated to our common good. (Just how He works in each individual is *His* choice!)

Actually, we Christians are the Body of Christ, many parts united as one. Like parts of the human body, we each have our own functions, as a "hand" or "foot" or "eye" or "ear." And we're each necessary; no one contribution should be singled out and exalted. So you're each in the Body, and *this* is what's important. But if we were to rank gifts by their importance, tongues would hardly be at the top of the list.

Really, there's a better way to attain true spirituality: love. No gift profits a person exercising it unless he loves. You want to measure spirituality? Then look to kindness, patience, and those other practical expressions of real love. For it is love that lifts us out of childhood; love is the mark of spiritual maturity.

Focus on love, and realize that the gifts used for communicating God's Word (prophecy) should have priority when you meet. You see, intelligible speech builds up our brother, and it is such building-up gifts that we should value. So, in church don't burst out in a tongue unless an interpretation can be given. And don't misunderstand! I speak in tongues more than you all; I'm not rejecting this gift. But I'd rather speak five words that will help someone than ten thousand words in a tongue no one can understand.

So get over your childish preoccupation with tongues. Tongues are certainly *not* meant to be a sign of special spirituality within the Body; as that kind of sign, their only appeal might be to pagans, as an indication of God's presence.

In church meetings let each one participate—but no more disorderly clamor! Take turns. God's work is marked by order, and you *can* control yourselves. As for the women who've been disrupting your meetings, they especially need to learn submissiveness. Tell them to be quiet in church and to discuss their questions with their husbands at home.

And if anyone there still wants to claim a "special spirituality," let him recognize the fact that I speak with God's own authority. So, brothers, don't forbid tongues, but do concentrate on communicating God's Word in your meetings.

Several points within this extended passage have been disputed or discussed. Some are very important in tracing the apostle's thought and, in fact, their interpretation may hinge on the grasp of the entire argument when more than one option is open. Here are observations that may be helpful:

*Prophecy (12:10).* The basic emphasis in Old and New Testaments is not on prediction but on setting forth clearly what God has said. In the New Testament church, *prophecy* indicates (1) a gift and/or (2) an office associated with the authoritative expression of God's message.

It's best always to associate prophecy with Scripture, either as an exposition of it or as being subject to Scripture for authentication.

*Seek the best gifts (12:31)*. This is not an exhortation for individuals to ask the Spirit for any particular gift. Instead, it is an exhortation to the church, because their attention had been drawn to "tongues" and they had actually ignored the more important ministries of the Spirit.

*A more excellent way (12:31)*. The Corinthians had made two mistakes. First, they had taken a spectacular but less significant spiritual gift and given it priority in their meetings (see chap. 14). Second, they'd carried over the pagan notion that such ecstatic utterance is a mark of spirituality—of special closeness to God. First Corinthians 13 deals with this second issue. How *do* we recognize special closeness to God in ourselves or others? All too often we yearn for a closer walk with the Lord. If we do not understand the closer walk, we're likely to grasp at an unusual experience such as tongues as the key. We're likely to listen to the person with the special experience as an authority and to mistake his gift as a divine mark of favor.

Paul wanted the believers to recognize the priority of the more important gifts, but he also wanted them to see that the key to spirituality is *completely unrelated* to the gifts a person may have from the Spirit. After all, Paul identified the Corinthian church as "still worldly" (3:3), yet there was an exercise of *all* the spiritual gifts in that body (1:7)!

The "more excellent way" is the way to a deeper walk with God. *Love* is the key to our growth toward maturity, and love is the indication (a practical indication, according to 13:4-7) of true spirituality in others.

*The church assembled (chap. 14).* With the principles explained in chapters 12 and 13, Paul then moved to apply them to the church gatherings. Apparently these assemblies had become a bedlam. Brothers and sisters were shouting out in tongues at the same time; prophecy was discounted, and the prophet often interrupted; and apparently a group of women had become very aggressive about their gift of tongues. Paul told the church to correct these abuses. All believers could contribute—and tongues were not to be forbidden!—but there were certain rules to be followed. God is a God of order. Anyone who claimed to have been just "swept away" by the Spirit and not to have been able to refrain from jumping up out of turn was not acting by the Spirit. As for those women who had become so aggressive and dominating, they had better learn to be quiet in church and discuss things with their husbands at home. Submission is a principle each of them needed to apply for her own growth and discipline—and for the sake of the church.

How like Paul. Even the greatest doctrines of the faith have the most practical implications.

*A sign to unbelievers? (14:20-25).* This is one of the most discussed passages in Scriptures, and there are several explanations of why Paul seems first to say that tongues are for and then not for outsiders. One explanation is this:

In the Greek culture, ecstatic utterances were taken as signs of the divine presence. Paul observed that unbelievers may view tongues as signs, even though believers were *not* to take them as a sign of spirituality (v. 22).

But such signs have a limited impact on the unsaved! If an unbeliever should attend a Christian meeting and see everyone shouting out in tongues, his impression is likely to be, "What a madhouse!" (see v. 23). But if he comes to a meeting and hears the Word of God in plain talk, he'll be convicted by the Spirit and converted (vv. 24-25).

The point is, then, that while outsiders may come to a Christian meeting because they have heard about a miraculous sign, seeing the sign in action won't lead to conversion. That requires a presentation of core truth in an understandable way.

*Summary.* Paul has given us vital and clear teaching about an issue that divides believers today just as it troubled the early church. In this passage we find no license to reject the gift of tongues as a valid manifestation of the Holy Spirit. At the same time, we find a corrective to an overemphasis on this gift, which would attempt to make it *the* evidence of God's Spirit's presence and *the* test of spirituality.

Once again Paul has gently and delicately guided the Corinthians, and us, to affirm a brother who differs from us, and has again lifted up the vital place of love.

BIBLE ALIVE SERIES

## THE BODY
*1 Corinthians 12*

*Family* is a very appropriate term. It's often used in the Bible. It communicates clearly the relationship of love and intimacy that is to mark the fellowship of believers. As sons and daughters of God now through our relationship with Jesus, we are also brothers and sisters. Learning to look at each other and think of ourselves as family helps us sense the warmth that is to be the mark of Christ's people.

Now Paul has introduced a new term which focuses on function. *Family* speaks of relationships; *body* speaks of ministry. And, particularly as we go on in our next book of the **Bible Alive Series,** we need to grasp the fact that we are a ministering people.

These two pictures of Christ's church are never held up in contrast. Instead, they are two perspectives on the same reality. For the *family relationship* is the *context for ministry.* And *ministry* is the contribution that love leads each of us to make to our fellow family members.

*The Head.* The picture of the body also helps us see how Jesus continues to perform His work in our world. As the "Head" of a living "body," Jesus directs us—we who are His hands and feet and eyes and ears and mouth—to continue His own mission in our world. The compassion Jesus showed to the sick and weary and the sin-tormented, He still shows—through His body! When we as individuals and local groups of believers mature and become sensitive to the Lord's guidance, Christ ministers to us and through us.

*Fellow members.* Paul develops the analogy of the body in this passage to teach us about our relationship with each other. We are *dependent* on each other. No one person is fully equipped with all the spiritual gifts. Instead, each is given his own distinctive gift or gifts; each then makes his own unique contribution to "the common good" (12:7).

It is through cooperation and coordination that each of us makes his contribution and, in turn, is helped and aided to grow. Individualism, with its emphasis on competition to discover the "best" and "greatest," is *totally foreign to the body of Christ.* The whole spirit of the Corinthian church was individualistic; they exalted favorite leaders, they competed doctrinally, they even competed to be given special individual "honor" because of the gift possessed. They were unable to see that each person needed the other and that they were *interdependent,* not independent.

How much we need to rediscover the reality of the body of Christ today! For our age, too, is ruggedly individualistic. We, too, exalt competitiveness and individual achievement. We, too, find it hard to work with others in a team relationship. But we *are* a body. And it is as a body—honoring each part, ministering and being ministered to—that we must learn to live in Jesus' family.

The more excellent way to experiencing life in Christ's body is that very way Paul marks out in 1 Corinthians 13: love.

BIBLE ALIVE SERIES

## GOING DEEPER

*to personalize*
1. Was your paraphrase summary of this passage significantly different from the author's? If so, go back and ask yourself why. Here are some questions that will help you analyze:
- What assumptions did you have when you started reading?
- How important in grasping the train of thought was the background information on tongues from the rest of the New Testament?
- How important in tracing the train of thought was the background information about the Hellenistic attitude toward ecstatic experiences?
- Did you rush over elements of the passage that puzzled you without trying to understand them? If so, which were they?

Can you gather any principles for Bible study from your responses to these questions?

2. Here is a series of statements about spiritual gifts and spirituality. Which would you identify as true and which false, and what evidence in the Bible text would you cite?

*The more important the spiritual gift a person has, the more mature and spiritual he must be.*

*Tongues is the main evidence of the Holy Spirit's presence in a person's life.*

*Tongues is definitely not for our day and age and should not be permitted in our fellowship.*

*We are supposed to ask God for the specific spiritual gift we want.*

*When a person is "under the influence" of the Holy Spirit, he just can't help shouting right out.*
*No woman should ever say anything in a meeting of believers.*
*It is impossible to recognize spirituality.*
*Some Christians don't have anything to contribute to others.*
*In church meetings, only the pastor is to teach, because he's usually the only one with seminary training.*

3. Think about your own congregation for a minute, and then answer these questions:
- Who are the most gifted people in your church? (List first names or initials.)
- Who are the most spiritual people in your church? (List first names or initials.)
- What made you choose the people on each list? Are the same names on each? What conclusions might you draw from this about your local church's understanding of the truths Paul presents in this passage?

4. Which teaching in this passage has the most practical significance to you? Why?

*to probe*

1. Do research on any of the issues raised in these chapters which still puzzle or concern you. And write a brief report.

*Note:* Because of the relative shortness of the two chapters of 1 Corinthians we'll examine next, you need *not* study the passages before reading the text discussion.

# 9
*1 Corinthians 7, 11*

# WOMEN IN THE CHURCH

IT MAY BE HARD to grasp at first, but it's true: Paul's ministry stimulated one of the first Women's Lib movements! Christian truth provided the basis for the affirmation of each woman's personal worth and value.

The impact of this discovery, and the struggle to understand the implications of lifting women up to stand beside men rather than crouching in their shadow, is reflected in the questions now posed for Paul's solution.

So many of the contemporary cries of the women's movement are reflected in these passages, and so many of the modern calls for action repeat the same calls shouted out then. First-century Christian women campaigned for the right to attend public worship with uncovered heads. Some of them disrupted the meetings by noisily challenging those who taught.

In Paul's handling of the questions in these two

chapters, we're helped to see God's unique answer, an answer that affirms the full personhood of women and gently guides us away from drawing false implications as to what that full personhood means.

## WOMEN IN THE BIBLE

It's important first to notice the Bible's consistent attitude toward women. Genesis 1 affirms the full personhood of Eve and her full participation in God's image as it is stamped on humankind. Eve also shares fully in the unique position of "dominion" God intended man to exercise over His whole creation.

> So God created man in his own image, in the image of God he created him; male and female he created them. And God . . . said to them, "Be fruitful . . . and have dominion."
> *Genesis 1:27, 28 (RSV)*

With sin, a new necessity was imposed on the race. Woman was assigned a subordinate place, just as later the destructive nature of man's sinful impulses forced the imposition of government on society (compare Gen. 3:16; 9:6 with Romans 13:1-4). This subordination implied no demeaning of women. It made a woman no less important than her husband as a person—just as today a mayor, governor, or even president is no more important as a person than the citizen. Romans 13 insists that the rulers' role is in fact to serve the citizen, and this is exactly the implication of Genesis 3 regarding the husband's authority.

But sin has a way of warping everything in our lives. Just as governments tend to become tyrannies, so "submission" became a denial of worth; "authority" became the right to use and discard. Rather than upholding the worth of women, divine order has been accused of denying it.

In Old Testament days, most cultures viewed women as chattels; they were denied rights commonly granted men and could be treated any way their husbands or owners pleased. It is probably difficult to realize now, but the Old Testament laws relating to women were significantly more liberal and supportive of women's rights than those in the rest of the world. Not that the Old Testament laws reflect the full restoration of women. Many Old Testament laws do *not* reflect God's ideal. They are accommodations to man's "hardness of heart," an adjustment of divine principles to the capacity of men to respond. (See the discussion of Matt. 19 in *The Servant King,* the first New Testament book in the **Bible Alive Series.)**

But even in the Old Testament, there were indications that God would act one day to reaffirm woman's position *beside* and not beneath man.

With Christ, those promised days came! One of the most dramatic transformations was in men's attitude toward women and in women's understanding of themselves. We see it so often throughout the Word:

> There is neither Jew nor Greek, slave nor free, male or female, for you are all one in Christ Jesus.
> *Galatians 3:28*

The old ways of valuing and classifying people are no longer valid! In Christ we are members of one Body.

> "I will pour out my Spirit upon all people.
> Your sons and your daughters will prophesy."
> *Acts 2:17*

Since the Spirit's coming on Pentecost, *every* member of the Body has been given a gift and called to minister. Even the gift of prophecy, which Paul identifies as very important (1 Cor. 12:27-30), is shared by women!

> I commend to you our sister Phoebe, a deaconess of the church at Cenchreae . . . she has been a helper of many and of myself.
> *Romans 16:1 (RSV)*

Paul not only valued women, but he recognized them as eligible to hold office in the church. In the same context he calls Priscilla and Aquila "my fellow workers in Christ" (v. 3).

It is difficult to see how some charge Paul with a narrow Pharisaic attitude toward women, or insist that the New Testament documents maintain a degrading, culture-bound view of the place of women in marriage and in the church. It was exactly because the early church *rejected* society's view of women that the Corinthian problem arose. Paul's guidelines here are not designed to put women "back in their place" but to help newly liberated women find their identity as persons of worth and value ... and to help men, stunned by this sudden recognition of women as God's ministers in the Body of Christ, to explore the implications of the new relationship.

## MARRIAGE PROBLEMS
*1 Corinthians 7*

In every age there are twin tendencies to distort the search for a depth relationship with the divine. One of these is asceticism, the notion that by rigorous denial of bodily drives and desires one attains special holiness. The other is licentiousness, often rooted in the belief that the physical does not matter and that, therefore, full expression of any passion is acceptable.

Paul had devastated this second view while in Corinth, and he repeated his condemnation of immorality in this letter (1 Cor. 5). It's clear that some had carried over the playboy philosophy of Corinth into the church, continuing to regard women as men's playthings.

But others had taken the ascetic route. The affirmation of women as sisters in Christ, with full rights in the body of believers, tended to encourage this thinking. If women are to be regarded fully as persons now (and not just as *female),* doesn't it follow that marriage and the physical side of sex should be ruled out? This notion stimulated the issue the Corinthians raised in this area when they reported to the apostle the affirmation "It is good for a man not to marry" (7:1).

Looking over an outline of the passage, we can see the kinds of marriage questions that were troubling the Corinthian church.

| | |
|---|---|
| 7:1-9 | Does women's full equality rule out marriage? |
| 7:10-11 | What about divorce? |
| 7:17-24 | A BASIC PRINCIPLE |
| 7:25-38 | What about our virgin daughters and engaged couples? |
| 7:39-40 | Any word for the widows? |

*1 Corinthians 7:1-9.* As was his practice, Paul begins by commending. It *is* "good for a man not to marry." But immediately he corrects a misinterpretation of this statement (which he himself probably made when with them; see v. 7). "Good" is *not* the same as "morally required" or even "better." In fact, marriage is the normal state. And marriage means *marriage*—with its full sexual expression. The "holy marriage" of celibacy that some would promote is not marriage at all. Full humanity involves the body and bodily needs; Christian couples are not to deprive one another sexually (v. 5). And in Christian marriage, it is not only the man who has rights and needs and desires. The woman has them as well, and she "owns" her husband's body as much as he "owns" hers.

What a devastating break with the culture! Full sexual equality and partnership make up an early

Christian teaching that must have jolted the believers' thinking then as it does the thinking of some now.

*1 Corinthians 7:10-11.* To those Christians who for any reason were initiating divorce action, Paul passes on this blunt command: "No." Should this teaching of Jesus be rejected, the divorced person must remain unmarried or be reconciled.

The fact that Paul clearly has the wife in mind here suggests that some of the newly liberated women in Corinth felt that to "find themselves" they had to step out of the "bondage" of marriage. Sometimes a sudden rediscovery that a woman is a person in her own right does lead to a desire to build her identity apart from old relationships and the "restrictions" of marriage. Paul makes it clear that this is not the way, but he seems to recognize that some women will divorce in spite of his injunction. In that case, he insists, either remain unmarried or be reconciled to your husband.

Almost as an afterthought, Paul seems to add, "By the way, you men aren't to divorce your wives either." Clearly the divorce question was stimulated by actions taken by women rather than men, and this leads us to suspect that the "Women's Lib" movement was the cause.

*1 Corinthians 7:12-16.* Even if a believer's spouse is not a Christian, the believer is not to initiate divorce. Christ's presence in the believer reaches out to touch the unbelieving family members; spouse and children are "sanctified" (v. 14) in this way, in the sense of being privileged to experience the influence of Jesus through the believer.

At the same time, if the *unbeliever* initiates a divorce, the Christian partner need not feel guilty about it. In fact, when this happens, the believer is not "bound" (under obligation). The marriage is dissolved.

*1 Corinthians 7:17-24.* Paul now speaks to a basic issue underlying most of these queries. In each case the believers seem to be seeking to find themselves or some special identity by *changing the conditions* under which they live. A wife wants to get a divorce so she can find her identity. A man wants to make his marriage "spiritual" by removing sex. To them and to us Paul replies, "Each one should retain the place in life that the Lord assigned to him and to which God has called him" (7:17).

God *is* sovereign.

God has *assigned us* our place.

God has *called us* to live in that place.

The newly liberated women in Corinth will not find themselves by seeking emancipation or in trying to be like men. Instead, identity and fulfillment will be found in living out their calling as women and as servants of the Lord. A slave's self-identity does not hinge on his being free. Possessing freedom doesn't make the freedman any less Christ's slave. A Jew shouldn't deny his cultural background and heritage, and a Gentile needn't deny his (vv. 18, 19). Instead, each of us is to bend every effort to live for Christ in the state in which we are called.

It is in serving and loving God *as we are* that we discover our real selves and find our fulfillment.

*1 Corinthians 7:25-38.* Paul's advice to parents concerned about arranging marriages for their unmarried daughters (which was the practice then) and to betrothed couples was to put off marriage "because of the present crisis" (v. 26). In that particular crisis situation—about which we know little today—concern for husband or wife might threaten the believer's commitment to God. (For instance, it is easier for most of us to face martyrdom and torture than to permit the torment of the members of our family.)

Still, Paul lets the believer know that God will guide differently in individual cases; they will not sin if they marry. After Paul's defense of marriage in the opening paragraph of this chapter, it's clear he does *not* hold an ascetic or puritanical view!

*1 Corinthians 7:39-40.* As for widows, of course, they are free to remarry—but only other Christians. And Paul says they might well be happier if they do not marry just now (contrast 1 Tim. 5:14).

And so Paul moves on in chapters 8—10 to another subject. But he will return again to problems that arose out of the restoration of women to full personhood. When he does, his argument will be founded on the principle stated here in 7:17.

*We find fulfillment in being who and what we are.*
God is sovereign.
He has assigned us our place.
God has, in fact, called us to live in that place.
Affirming the worth and value of who we are, not struggling to be something we are not, is the secret of fulfillment.

# 1 CORINTHIANS 11

The subjects taken up in this chapter deal with public worship. The first focuses on several practices of the Christian women's liberation party. The second relates to the practice of Communion. It is the first of these we want to concentrate on.

Paul begins by praising the believers—including the women—for holding to his previous teachings (v. 2). He then goes on to answer those who have challenged these.

Again we need to sketch some cultural background before looking at the passage itself. What really is at issue in the Corinthian women's desire to dispense with the veil (to go "uncovered") in public worship?

*The veil covering.* Sir William Ramsey gives us some insight into the cultural implications of the evil:

> In Oriental lands the veil is the power and the honour and dignity of the woman. With the veil on her head she can go anywhere in security and profound respect. She is not seen; it is a mark of thoroughly bad manners to observe a veiled woman in the streets. She is alone. The rest of the people around are non-existent to her, as she is to them. She is supreme in the crowd.... But without the veil the woman is a thing of nought, whom any man may insult.... A woman's authority and dignity vanish along with the all-covering veil that she discards.[1]

The veil served to affirm the woman's dignity *as a woman.*

Why did the Corinthian ladies want to remove their veils in the church meetings? Because they felt a need to symbolize their new status as full participants in the Body of Christ. If they were equals to men, they wanted to be like men and to worship unveiled.

Paul's response is not a put-down. Instead, it is a reaffirmation of the fact that a woman can be valuable and worthwhile *as a woman*. No woman needs to seek liberation by struggling to become like men.

*An inappropriate symbol.* It's significant here that Paul does not argue, as he might have, from the cultural implication of going unveiled. In that society, the discrete matron would demonstrate her propriety in the way she dressed, while the *heterai* "available for hire") would advertise herself by her dress. Surely Paul could have taken the approach of shaming them for acting like harlots.

But he does not. Instead, he affirms them. He argues that there *are* differences between men and women, and that it is no disgrace to recognize the difference. Acting in ways appropriate for a woman in no way denies the Christian woman's worth and value, and it in no way threatens her participation in the Body of Christ.

*An unnecessary demand.* In verses 2—16 Paul explains that there *are* differences between men and women that are to be recognized. But the differences are designed to make men and women *interdependent* rather than to make one of them of lesser importance.

Paul's argument here is a theological one, finding

its roots in the order of creation. The man does have a certain priority; he was created first, and woman was shaped from his flesh. Eve was created to meet Adam's need for companionship rather than vice versa. This order in creation is reflected in the relationship between a man and his wife. He is the "head" of the woman, even as Christ is the head of man.

Usually it is at this point that the modern person rebels. *Head,* to most of us means *authority,* and in our day, *authority* connotes suppression and oppression. But note that this is not the way Paul views it here. Man is "the image and glory" of God (v. 7). *Rather than indicating oppression by God, the Lord's headship over man implies the exaltation of man!*

So, too, with the woman. Man's headship over the woman does not imply subservience, but instead the lifting up of the woman. Headship does not proclaim the right of men to enslave women. Just the opposite. It insists that men should recognize the high value God places on woman not only as fully a person but as man's "glory!" Thus, in wearing a veil (that "sign of authority"), the Corinthian women would be displaying for men and angels as well the stunning fact that in Christ it is no shame to be female. Each time they participated *as a woman* in the ministry of the church, they would show again the value, worth, and glory of womankind.

In verses 11-16 Paul does make a cultural appeal. At that time long hair *was* womanly, and men would be ashamed to let theirs grow long. Would a woman ever think of shaving her head and appearing in public without her hair? Of course not! She'd be ashamed. Why? Because somehow, without long hair, she would be denying her femininity.

So, Paul says, it really isn't proper to appear in church and to pray unveiled either. For this, too, is a denial of femininity. A woman would be denying herself—not finding herself—by attempting to become like a man.

## ECHOES

It's here we find echoes of the principle stated in chapter 7. We find fulfillment in being who and what we are.

God is sovereign.

He has assigned each of us our place.

He has called us to live in that place.

This is the message that echoes from those first-century days to our own. In tones of love, the great apostle reminded women who were breaking out of old, distorted feelings of worthlessness and unimportance that it was not necessary to deny their womanhood in order to find their new identity. Rather, they would find it in accepting themselves as women and glorying in that fact. For a woman *is* important, not *in spite* of being a woman, but *as one*.

## GOING DEEPER

*to personalize*

1. Study 1 Corinthians 7 and 11:2-16 carefully.
2. Why do you think women in our society today

speak of "liberation"? What do you feel women want? Have women been deprived of their rights as persons? How?

3. What about women in the church today? Have women been denied their rights as persons? What do you think is the general attitude toward the place of women in the church? What do you think it should be?

4. There are other passages relating to women in the church, some of which seem more difficult to understand than these. Keeping in mind the background and the argument developed in this chapter, how would you understand each reference below? Are you satisfied with the following explanations? Why, or why not?

*1 Corinthians 14:33-36.* In this passage on church disorders, Paul is not saying to women, "Stifle yourselves." He is warning aggressive Women's Libbers to stop shouting and interrupting with their argumentative questions. They should instead talk things over with their husbands at home, and in the process learn a submission that's appropriate for them as women.

*1 Timothy 2:11-15.* This does not mean that women can't exercise their gifts when the body meets, but, instead, it specifically focuses on a role—that of the ruling elder. To "teach" (v. 12), and this is specified as teaching "with authority," is an elder's function. This particular function—and only this function—in the Body of Christ is reserved for men.

5. If the above interpretation is correct, and

women are not to be elders:
— Does this indicate that women are inferior?
— Does this indicate that women are not really "equal" to men?
— Does "equal" mean "the same in every way"?
— Does this mean a woman should not preach in church?
— Does this mean that a woman should not share what God has shown her in the Scripture at church meetings?
— Does this mean that men who are not elders are inferior to those who are?

*to probe*

1. How many references to women can you find in Paul's writings? Examine each, and see if you can find additional evidence of his attitude toward them.

2. Check through a number of commentaries on the passages in question. Are other interpretations suggested? What observations by the commentators help you understand this important area of women in the church?

3. Skim at least three books about women written by Christian women. How do they handle these Corinthian chapters? What seems to be their attitude toward Paul? Toward themselves as women?

---

1. Cited in Archibald Robertson and Alfred Plummer, *Corinthians One,* 2nd ed., International Critical Commentary (Naperville, Ill., Allenson, 1914), p. 311.

# 10

*1 Corinthians 15–16*

# RESURRECTION!

CHRIST PROMISED TRANSFORMATION.
And there *was* transformation.
Believers found striking changes were taking place—within themselves, and in one another. The attitudes and ideas and ways of paganism died hard. Yet, there was still clear evidence of God's work within the Corinthian body.

In spite of differences and divisions, and in spite of laxity in discipline, people were delivered from superstition and fear. The bondage of idolatry was shattered; an exciting new freedom was experienced. God's presence with them was abundantly demonstrated; all the spiritual gifts were operating in the body, and they were excited about each new experience of the Spirit. Their attitudes and values were changing, too. They took very seriously Paul's teachings on marriage—and even went beyond them in some cases.

The believers appealed to Scripture and God's

Word for guidance (through the apostolic teaching), and were praised for holding to the practices Paul taught them. Women were breaking out of their position of servitude, rejoicing in their liberation, and asserting themselves in bold (if sometimes misdirected) ways. In general, the Corinthians seemed very responsive to truth; Paul always expected that they would respond obediently to his instructions.

Each of these facts gives witness that transformation had begun. These believers *were* changing and growing, becoming new and different persons.

At the same time, their growth was retarded, apparently because of a lack of that vital quality Paul spoke of so often in writing to the Thessalonians. To the church in Thessalonica he could say, "About brotherly love we do not need to write to you, for you yourselves have been taught by God to love each other" (1 Thess. 4:9). But to the Corinthians, Paul had to say, "Knowledge puffs up, but love builds up" (1 Cor. 8:1), and then go on to show them how to handle their differences lovingly. It was to the Corinthians that the great exposition of love in 1 Corinthians 13 was addressed, and one of Paul's last reminders to them was, "Do everything in love" (16:14).

*A process.* All this helps us realize again that growing toward Christian maturity is a process. God does work His transformation of our personalities, but that work takes place over a period of time, and sometimes over more time than we desire!

Sometimes growth seems slow as we face problems like those that plagued the church at Corinth.

We need to keep three things in mind. First, as newness comes, there always will be tension between the old and new ways. The transition time is sure to bring problems.

Second, building the climate of love in the body will ease the tensions. Love, like truth, is essential. By affirming our oneness with other believers as Christ's Body, by affirming our love for each other in spite of differences and strains, and by affirming together our commitment to truth, we *will* grow. We are being freed from the world's mold—that old way of thinking, of valuing, and of perceiving ourselves and others. We are being transformed in a process to which God has committed Himself. Words Paul would later pen to encourage the Philippians hold a promise to the Corinthians—and to us—as well: "He who began a good work in you will carry it on to completion until the day of Christ Jesus" (Phil. 1:6).

And this brings us to the third thing. A day of completion is coming! In the day of Christ Jesus, our transformation will be complete.

## RESURRECTION

Some in Corinth denied this completion. Carrying over the typical Greek attitude toward life after death, they could not accept the idea of a bodily resurrection. Christian faith might have meaning in the temporal present, they felt. It might even offer them some astral form for their personalities following physical death. But, a *literal* resurrection?

Paul vigorously corrects them. If our only hope is

related to this life, then we Christians are "of all men most miserable" (1 Cor. 15:19, KJV). Transformation begins in the present, but completion will come in the day of Christ Jesus. Then we will actually "bear the likeness of the man from heaven" (v. 49). What God does in our earthly lives not only excites us, it holds the glittering prospect of perfection to come. The transformation process finds its ultimate meaning in attaining its goal.

It *is our* destiny to *be like* Jesus.

Moreover, the Good News of Jesus rests on the fact of the Lord's resurrection. He was raised bodily from the dead. His resurrection both demonstrates the power of God and is the ultimate proof of His ability to provide forgiveness. Jesus' resurrection and ours are so intimately intertwined that to doubt either constitutes a denial of the gospel message itself.

Eager to explain this vital truth, Paul, in 1 Corinthians 15, gives the classic and definitive New Testament explanation of resurrection.

*1 Corinthians 15:1-11.* Paul insists that the doctrine is absolutely basic truth (v. 2), and that the fact of Jesus' resurrection was attested by many witnesses, all of whom, like Paul, proclaimed it as a core Christian truth.

*1 Corinthians 15:12-19.* The resurrection of the believer is linked to that of Jesus. Both are true, and literally so, or neither is. "If Christ has not been raised, your faith is futile; you are still in your sins" (v. 17). And to be pitied for an empty hope!

*1 Corinthians 15:20-28.* In fact, Christ *has* been

raised from the dead. God's whole plan hinges on resurrection, and God *does* have a plan. The death that entered the world with Adam's sin has been reversed, and believers have been made alive in Christ. In God's time, the end will come. Jesus will establish God the Father's dominion, and then the last enemy—death itself—will be destroyed.

*1 Corinthians 15:29-34.* Between thirty and forty explanations have been given for "baptized for the dead" in verse 29. The simple meaning of the words seems to suggest that some at Corinth were undergoing baptism on behalf of friends who died without that sacrament. In referring to the practice, Paul does not endorse it. In fact, he disassociates himself from it by referring to "those" people and "they" rather than "we."

It's clear that in both cases mentioned in this paragraph Paul is reasoning from Christian experience rather than revelation. Why bother to undergo such a baptism if your friends are simply dead and gone and there is no resurrection? Why should the missionary team with Paul keep on endangering their lives if death is really the end? If this life is all, why not live by that contemporary maxim "Eat and drink, for tomorrow we die" (v. 32)?

No, it is the prospect of the final transformation that causes the Corinthians' peculiar practice and Paul's continued commitment.

Paul's point in verses 33 and 34 is that wandering from the truth about resurrection will certainly have an impact on daily life. The loss of hope will rob us of commitment.

*1 Corinthians 15:35-49.* It was natural in the debate over resurrection that some should inquire, "Well, what will this resurrection body be like, anyway?" And that others should challenge, "How can men rise when their bodies have decayed?" Paul replies, "How foolish!" (v. 36). A dead-looking seed is planted in the ground, and a vital, living plant appears. Just as God gives the planted seed the body appropriate to its new life, so the resurrected saint will have a glorious body appropriate to full transformation.

No, the resurrection body will not be the same body we have now; natural life will be replaced by spiritual. The likeness we bear then will not be Adam's, but, instead, "we shall bear the likeness of the man from heaven" (v. 49).

*1 Corinthians 15:50-57.* Paul is now caught up in a great vision of that future day. He sees the dead being raised, and the living caught up—transformed! In glory and splendor the perishable fades and mortality is clothed with immortality. And then—then comes his triumphant shout.

"Death has been swallowed up in victory" (v. 54).

*1 Corinthians 15:58.* What are Paul's last words on this vital subject? *As you live your life now, keep your ultimate transformation in clear view:*

Therefore, my dear brothers, stand firm. Let nothing move you. Always give yourselves fully to the work of the Lord, because you know that your labor in the Lord is not in vain.

This life is *not* the end. Labor "in the Lord" is not in vain. The great day of transformation is on the way.

## GOING DEEPER

*to personalize*

1. Read 1 Corinthians 15 carefully, and the farewells in chapter 16 as well.
2. In the text the author briefly discusses both our progressive transformation and the ultimate transformation to be ours in the resurrection. What relationships between the two (progressive and ultimate) aspects of transformation can you see? List as many as you can.
3. In Romans 8:18-39, Paul also discussed the impact of the ultimate transformation on our lives now. What in this passage seems particularly significant to you?
4. How real has been your own awareness of the coming resurrection? What impact has it had on your life? Or, what impact do you think a better understanding and grasp of this truth might have on your daily life?

*to probe*

It is important to master the content of Scripture as well as to explore its message. Often this involves memorization, which is not difficult or burdensome if what is memorized has real meaning to you. So far in this text the author has tried to guide you to explore these New Testament books for yourself

BIBLE ALIVE SERIES

and to focus on their meaning. It will be much more beneficial if you pause now to review what you've covered and to master the content of these significant chapters.

The chart on pages 135-36 is designed to help you in this mastery. Memorize it, and you'll have a tool to put these exciting days of the New Testament church in immediate perspective as well as to enrich your future study of these passages.

If you are taking this study as a course for credit, you can expect your exam to be based in part on this chart. Memorizing it will enable you to handle all test questions effectively.

Also, add principles that you think are important to the chart. Some that might be included have been purposely excluded. Make a careful search through both this textbook and the Scriptures for principles to add.

## THE CHURCH IN MISSION
*Acts 16–19; 1 and 2 Thessalonians; 1 Corinthians*

| Passage | Theme* | Principles |
|---|---|---|
| Acts 16—19 | Gospel Communication | Contextualize core truth. |
| 1 Thess. 1—2 | Love | Exemplify God's love in your relationships. |
| 1, 2 Thess. | Transformation | The community promises believers "newness-of-life" transformation. |
| 1 Cor. 1—4 | Overcoming Barriers to Divisions | Reject pagan approaches, seeking to understand God's patterns of thought. Regard human leaders as servants; reserve glory for God. |
| 1 Cor. 5—6 | Discipline | Deal firmly with sin in the family. Act to resolve disputes equitably. |
| 1 Cor. 8—10 | Doctrinal Disputes | Love and truth are both required for resolution. Being "right" does not remove love's obligation to build up our brothers. |

| Passage | Theme* | Principles |
|---|---|---|
| 1 Cor. 12—14 | True Spirituality | Possession of certain gifts is not evidence of spiritual achievement. Love is the key indicator of spiritual maturity As a body, family members are interdependent; each gift is important, and each person's ministry is needed. |
| 1 Cor. 7, 11 | Women's Identity | Affirm the worth and value of women. Equality as persons does not mean "sameness." Each person finds fulfillment in the role God has sovereignly chosen for him or her—and is *called* to that place. Because women are affirmed as equally valued persons in the Body of Christ, no woman needs to deny her womanhood. |
| 1 Cor. 15 | Resurrection | Ultimate transformation is assured. |

*Be able to demonstrate these themes by reference to and explanation of specific verses and passages.

# 11

*2 Corinthians 1–4*

# THE INADEQUATE MAN

PAUL'S LETTER TO THE CORINTHIANS had a mixed reception. Many did respond. For instance, the brother living in immorality was turned around. Others bridled at Paul's gentle yet blunt teaching. It's clear from 2 Corinthians that some challenged Paul's authority and apostleship. They charged him with unwarranted pride and overconfidence, and with saying one thing one time and something else at another time. The recriminations from this segment of the church in Corinth were apparently furious and bitter—so serious that Paul had to express his deep love for and confidence in them.

While he intended to deal with several specific questions (such as financial giving), the main thrust of the letter seems to be to reassure the Corinthians that in spite of what Paul's enemies were saying, he did trust them completely and cared for them. His motives and feelings, as well as his teachings, had been twisted by his critics. For the Corinthians' own benefit, Paul opened his heart in complete self-revelation.

## UNNECESSARY?

Earlier Paul had written to the Thessalonians and referred to his motives. "You know how we lived among you for your sake," he said (1 Thess. 1:5; see also 2:5). Paul's whole approach to ministry was to live among the members of a new body as a completely transparent man. He freely and openly expressed his motives, his feelings, his values—everything. Paul so loved his converts that he was ready to share with them not only the gospel but his own self as well.

Certainly he had been this kind of man with the Corinthians. There could be no reasonable basis for doubting him or questioning his motives. Yet a group in Corinth did question. Their backbiting and innuendoes were troubling the whole body of believers. Perhaps these were people converted after Paul had left Corinth, people who never knew him. Or perhaps they were simply proud and bitter people whose pretensions to superiority—whether based on claims of superior "knowledge" or on the supposed superiority of their tongues gift—had been gently destroyed by Paul's earlier letter. At any rate, they did attack Paul—bitterly. They could not refute his teaching, so they attacked the apostle personally, seeking to undermine his influence by making him appear to be a weak, plastic, venial man.

It should have been unnecessary for Paul to defend himself against this kind of attack. Many in Corinth had been converted under Paul's ministry. But apparently even they were shaken in their confidence in him, and in themselves. The weakness and failures Paul had identified in that first letter must have devastated the faithful; even they began to doubt if Paul could love and continue to respect them.

And so, Paul wrote 2 Corinthians—which should have been an unnecessary letter. But in this letter, Paul ministers in unique ways to us today. We find answers to some of the most basic questions about spiritual leadership facing the Church today. And we find in the self-revelation of Paul, a picture of the kind of person God is calling each of us to become.

## THE CONTRIBUTIONS OF 2 CORINTHIANS

What are some of the specific values we'll receive from our study of this book?

*Transformation.* Several times in the Corinthian letters Paul urged the young believers to "follow my example, as I follow the example of Christ" (1 Cor. 11:1). "Transformation" sounds like such an abstract thing. Even when we say that transformation involves growth in Christlikeness, it's hard for us to grasp the meaning. But in the person of Paul (a living, breathing, real human being whom the body could watch and observe and listen to), Christlikeness took on new meaning. In the close, personal relationship Paul developed with his converts, they could learn the life-style of one who had traveled further than they down transformation's road.

The invitation of Paul to believers to "imitate me" or to "let me be your example in this" was not rooted in pride. It was rooted in the apostle's awareness that a living example is essential in the communication of Christian truth. As we saw earlier (chap. 3, pp. 41-46), the bridge between God's truth and learning and receiving it is the modeling of that truth in an observable life.

This is one reason why 2 Corinthians is so important to us today. We don't know Paul as a person. We don't live in his first-century world. But in his letter, we not only meet Paul face to face, we meet him heart to heart. In this most intimate biblical portrayal of Paul as a person, we discover in him the kind of person God is calling us to become.

*Motivation.* In a recent nationwide survey of 5,000 pastors throughout the country conducted by Renewal Research Associates, a Phoenix, Arizona, foundation, *every respondent* when asked to identify the greatest needs in strengthening the life and ministry of his church gave first or second priority to "getting my lay people more involved as ministering men and women." The problem is motivation. How do we move others to follow Jesus? What is the *motivational key* to making disciples?

All too often we hear a presentation of the Scriptures that is cast in an "ought" framework. We're made to feel guilt or shame for what we haven't done, we're urged to try harder. Such guilt-producing approaches create a sense of hopelessness or helplessness, and actually retard transformation. At best, they force us into a flurry of activity that we mistake as "ministry."

God has a far better way, a far more freeing way!

In 2 Corinthians, we'll come to know Paul the motivator and discover a totally different avenue to discipleship.

*Authority.* A final focus in our exploration of this intimate letter will be authority. This, too, is a question troubling the Church today. What is the nature of spiritual authority? How is it exercised? How can we have authority that isn't oppressive, impersonal, restrictive—even degrading?

In observing Paul gently exercise his authority in the Corinthian church, we'll gain new insights into how Christian authority operates. In the process, we'll find guidance for our own lives in our homes and in the Church of God.

This New Testament letter is an exciting one! Once again, God's Word will speak to each one of us. In listening, we'll find new and open doorways to our personal growth toward the likeness of Jesus Christ.

## BIOGRAPHICAL BIBLE STUDY

So far in this study we've used two important Bible study methods: the *topical* (in which we examine a book or books of the Bible to see what is said about a specific theme or topic), and the *synthetic* (which involves tracing the thought of the writer over extended passages and synthesizing, or "putting it all together." Now we're going to use the biographical approach. Through this most intimate and personal of Paul's New Testament letters, we're going to try to come to know Paul, the man. We're going to read, to explore his motives, to clarify his values, to examine his every attitude, to sense his feelings and emotions, and to grasp the basic beliefs that shaped him as a person. In the process, we'll find out something of the kind of persons God is calling us to be. We'll gain a new appreciation for the fact that a Christian is not only someone who believes a certain way but is in addition a man or woman whose whole personality is touched by the Spirit of God.

The guide questions at the end of this and the following chapters will lead you into the biographical study approach. You'll not only learn from Paul as a person, but you'll also learn how to apply this method to connect other Bible characters.

We'll also see how the biographical method of Bible study can lead us to understand truth in ways we might not if we remained rigorously logical in our study. Truth in Scripture is *not* divorced from life. When seen in and through life, we often discover aspects of truth's meaning we would otherwise miss. This is particularly so about teachings such as authority. The "chain of command" structures that some people build reflect only one dimension of what spiritual authority involves. Unless viewed from a perspective that includes its *living expression,* our systems will always distort God's truth more than they reflect it.

*Truth in life.* Yet, it's important to remember that what we see in Scripture through the filter of life is actually rooted in truth. The living example of men like Paul does not have validity in itself; instead, the life-style is valid only when it expresses truth.

For instance, in this letter we'll meet Paul as vulnerable and inadequate. We'll see that Paul, under attack from the Corinthians, did not respond from a position of strength. Instead, he responded by revealing his weakness! At the very beginning of this letter he wrote, "We do not want you to be uninformed, brothers, about the hardships we suffered in the province of Asia. We were under great pressure, far beyond our ability to endure, so that we despaired of life itself. Indeed, in our hearts we felt the sentence of death" (2 Cor. 1:8, 9). How striking! Paul immediately exposed himself to his enemies.

How they might have used that against him! Can't you hear them now? "Paul's not so great. Look, he gets depressed just like a brand-new believer! Why, what does he know of victorious Christian living? He even admits feeling despair."

Or, "How can you ever respect a weak person like that? Paul needs help!"

Why did Paul give his enemies this kind of edge? Why didn't he simply exercise his great power as an apostle and judge the critics? Why didn't he at least begin by recounting his strengths rather than by revealing his weaknesses?

Paul's underlying motive for this approach was his desire to minister to the Corinthians. He knew that, to minister effectively, he would have to identify with them in their humanity before he could show them a way to rise beyond themselves. Paul also grasped a basic truth—and realized its full implications. In order to truly minister to others, you must be completely honest and real with them. Here's why.

*2 Corinthians 3:12-18.* In the context, Paul is speaking about transformation. God has chosen in Christ to write His Word, not on tablets of stone, but upon "tablets of human hearts" (3:2). Speaking about the glory of this ministry of transformation, Paul says an interesting thing:

> Therefore, since we have such a hope, we are very bold. We are not like Moses, who veiled his face to keep the Israelites from gazing at it while the radiance was fading away.
> *2 Corinthians 3:12-13*

What he's referring to is the time in the Old Testament when Moses received the Ten Commandments from God. When Moses came down from Mount Sinai, his face shone with a visible and brilliant radiance. The Old Testament tells us only that Moses then veiled his face. Paul, under the inspiration of the Spirit, tells us why.

Remember that Moses was leading a group of people much like some of the Corinthians. The Israelites were constantly challenging Moses' leadership. They murmured, complained, plotted against him, and at times were on the verge of stoning him to death! But when he came from Sinai with that visible spendor shining on his face, the people must have been stunned into temporary silence. We can even imagine Moses taking daily walks through the camp, thrilled by the reactions.

But one morning Moses noticed that the splendor was fading! The glow was going. And the Bible says, "Moses... veiled his face to keep the Israelites from gazing at it while the radiance was fading away" (3:13). A process of deterioration was taking place, and Moses couldn't bear to have others see it.

But ah, the contrast! Paul says, "We are very bold"! And he explains:

> Where the Spirit of the Lord is, there is freedom. And we, who with unveiled faces all reflect the Lord's glory, are being transformed into his likeness with ever-increasing glory, which comes from the Lord, who is the Spirit.
> 2 Corinthians 3:17-18

What is Paul saying? Simply this: I unveil and reveal myself in order that you might see Jesus in me. Jesus is not revealed in our "perfection" but in the progressive transformation of our experience, which can only be explained by His presence.

Paul revealed his weaknesses. But in doing so, he also revealed Jesus. Paul *was* weak, but the Spirit of God was constantly at work in him, working his transformation, overcoming his weaknesses, and infusing him with His strength. By taking off all the veils, Paul knew that they would not only meet Paul, the inadequate man, but that they *would also see Jesus.*

*Core truths.* How stunningly clear. In Paul's explanation of his openness and vulnerability, we see the meaning of several basic truths to which Scripture testifies:

- We are sinners, warped and twisted out of shape, far from being the persons we want to be or that God intended us to be.
- Jesus Himself enters the life of the believer; once born again, we receive "his own indestructible heredity" (1 Pet. 1:23, Phillips).
- God is *in the process* of working His transformation in us believers: we "are being transformed into his likeness with ever-increasing glory" (2 Cor. 3:18).

To Paul, the implications of these truths are compelling. As a leader, called to be an example, Paul had to take the veil off his life and personality and let others see him as he really was. Of course Paul realized that the Corinthians would discover his weaknesses; his transformation was incomplete. But Paul also realized that since Jesus was in his life, his brothers and sisters would also be "beholding the glory of the Lord" (2 Cor. 3:18, RSV). As they saw Jesus at work in Paul, they would find the confidence to hope for their own transforfmation.

It costs to be this kind of Christian. Some will misunderstand and try to use our weaknesses against us. Others will tend to look down on us. But once again Paul has opened for us God's way of thinking—a way so very different from man's. Not pride or self-protection, but humility and self-revelation. Paul's understanding of this truth led to his commitment: "We have renounced secret and shameful ways; we do not use deception, nor do we distort the word of God. On the contrary, by setting forth the truth plainly, we commend ourselves to every man's conscience in the sight of God" (2 Cor. 4:2).

May the Lord use Paul's example to free you and me to live and to minister in this same way.

## GOING DEEPER

*to personalize*

1. Read quickly the first four chapters of 2 Corinthians. Then jot down your impressions of Paul as a person. If you could choose one word to characterize him, what would it be? Why?

2. Reread these first four chapters slowly and carefully. Probe Paul's personality. What insights do you get into his motives?

    his values?
    his attitudes?
    his feelings?
    his thoughts?

What do you think was Paul's image of himself? How did he view others? God?

3. If Paul were asked to "tell us everything we need to know to understand you as a person" in 250 words, what do you think he would say? Write down, as though you were Paul, that explanation.

4. The author deals on pages 143-45 with Paul's openness, honesty, and vulnerability. How would you evaluate the following possible reactions to an exhortation that Christian leaders "be real"?

- "But, people will lose respect for me."
- "Exposing weakness like that must undermine authority."
- "It's all right, but it can be carried too far."

- "If you expose weaknesses, won't young Christians become discouraged and feel that Christ doesn't really offer hope of transformation?"
- "People today feel uncomfortable with all this 'personal' and 'self-revelation' stuff."

5. What implications can be found in pages 143-45 for parents in their relationship with their teenagers?

# 12

*1 Corinthians 5–9*

# "LIFE IS AT WORK IN YOU"

PAUL WAS NOT ONLY a great evangelist and teacher. He was a master motivator. In these chapters we see Paul at his best, and we discover the motivational keys that stimulate commitment to Jesus Christ in His Body, the Church.

Actually, we're given hints in the first four chapters. Perhaps you picked them up. They're found in phrases like these:
- "Our hope for you is firm" (1:7).
- "You help us by your prayers" (1:11).
- "We will boast of you in the day of the Lord Jesus" (1:14).
- "I was confident of this" (1:15).
- "I had confidence in all of you" (2:3).
- "Reaffirm your love for him" (2:8).

And, of course, the key phrase that I've taken as the title for this chapter: "Life is at work in you" (4:12).

How are these phrases related to motivation?

The football coach who chews out his players is doing it to motivate them. The parent who demands, "Sit down and do your homework *before* you go out," is seeking to motivate. The pastor who preaches a fiery sermon on coming judgment is seeking to use fear to motivate action.

We have so many ways of attempting to move people. We set goals for them and urge them to achieve. We make rules and insist that others keep them. We shame, urge, condemn, and plan competitions in the hope that *something* will move others to respond. The unhappy wife nags her husband, the disappointed parent belittles his child, and even the proud parent withholds praise in an effort to stimulate still higher achievement. And all of them wonder, at times, "Why?"

"Why doesn't my husband improve?"

"Why doesn't my child *try?*"

"Why don't members of our congregation get involved?"

The answer to all these questions is the same. It's because we're trying to use man's approach to moving others. As we've seen so often in 1 Corinthians, man's wisdom is not God's. God has His own unique and vital way of doing His work in our lives.

What are the elements in God's approach for moving believers to follow Jesus? One of the themes (repeated over and over again in these Epistles) is the example of the spiritual leader. Now we see two other factors, each of which is crucial in creating a climate that frees the individual to respond and to grow.

*Unconditional love.* This is the first motivational tool a Christian parent or leader has. And how often we see that kind of love stressed by Paul in this book.

Apparently Paul's first letter was taken by some of the Corinthians to indicate that Paul no longer loved them; they took his gentle explanation as "cold" reasoning. Over and over he reassured them: "We are not withholding our affection from you" (6:12).

Sometimes we hear psychologists suggest that to withdraw love is an effective way for parents to discipline their children. Far from it! In fact, it is the awareness of unconditional love—that sense of certainty that we are supported by a love that will never let us go—that creates a context for growth. Where there is uncertainty about love, there is also uncertainty about our personal worth and value; there is also fear of failure and the unwillingness to take a risk. It seems safer not to try, safer never to fail, safer never to risk the possible withdrawal of love.

Whatever we can say about man's approaches to motivation, about nagging, anger, shaming, chewing out, or demanding achievement, one thing is sure. They do *not* communicate unconditional love.

*Expectant confidence.* This was the second dimension of Paul's approach to motivation. He let the Corinthians know that he was confident they would grow. "I have great confidence in you," Paul said. "I take great pride in you. I am greatly encouraged; in all our troubles my joy knows no bounds" (7:4).

Here Paul was not writing to the Thessalonians, whose work of faith and labor of love and endurance inspired by hope was so abundantly plain. No, he was writing to the Corinthians, the church marked by division and marred by troublesome disputes.

It's easy to see how Paul might have expressed confidence in the Thessalonians—but the Corinthians? Yet, over and over he reassured them that he had confidence in them. And his confidence was not because of the Corinthians' achievement, but in spite of their lack of it!

While the Corinthians had begun to lose confidence in themselves, Paul strongly affirmed that his confidence was unshaken. Paul would believe in them—until they learned to believe in themselves.

This is the key. For growth, there must be hope. For motivation, there must be the confident expectation of success. That expectation cannot be based on performance. For no matter how we may try, our efforts are bound to fall short at times.

## THE BASIS OF HOPE

Paul's confident reassurance of the Corinthians was not a way of manipulating them. It was not a technique. Instead, Paul was sharing with these uncertain and ashamed believers what he really felt about them.

Such an expression of confidence, if it is honest, cannot be based on past performance. If our hope for ourselves or others is based on performance, there's bound to be a growing sense of discouragement and the ultimate loss of hope.

This is one of the traps parents often fall into with their children. Time after time they instruct or encourage or request. And time after time their child fails to respond. He doesn't do his homework. He forgets to make his bed. He neglects chores. He keeps on resisting correction. He won't confess mistakes, no matter how gently or firmly you deal with him. Before long, the parent's confidence is worn away. Before long, the parent *expects* the child to disappoint him. And the child, sensing the parent's attitude, also begins to expect himself to fail.

And he proceeds to live by those expectations.

So it's important to learn Paul's secret. It's important that we learn how to build confidence and hope in others by maintaining confidence in them ourselves.

*2 Corinthians 5:11-21.* To understand this passage, we must realize first that Paul is not talking about evangelism when he speaks of the "ministry of reconciliation" (v. 18). "Reconciliation" literally means to "bring into harmony." When we set our watch by the electric clock in the kitchen, we are "reconciling" our watch to the clock, changing one so that it keeps time by the standard set by the other. This is what Paul wants for the Corinthians: to bring their lives into harmony with the pattern set by God.

Paul points out that it's only appropriate that we live by the heartbeat of God's life rather than the old heartbeat of humankind. Since Jesus loved and died for believers, they should "no longer live for themselves, but for him who died for them and was raised again" (v. 15). As they do, they will "become the righteousness of God" in Him (v. 21).

It is this goal of leading believers to live in full

harmony with God's righteousness that Paul has in mind when he says, "We implore you on Christ's behalf: Be reconciled to God" (v. 20).

Paul begins by assuring the Corinthians that his expressions of confidence in them are no insincere attempt at flattery (vv. 11, 12). Yet how can he have confidence in them and criticize their behavior at the same time? In explaining, Paul demonstrates how different his approach is from those whose confidence rests only on performance, who "take pride in what is seen rather than in what is in the heart" (v. 12).

And this, of course, is the key! Paul's confidence is not based on what the Corinthians have done but on what God, who is in their hearts, has committed Himself to do!

See the train of thought. Christ's love within will "compel" (motivate) us. The reality is that in Christ we died. Now alive, we are freed to live for Him and not bound to ourselves (vv. 14, 15). Jesus' death was for the purpose of making it possible for us to live for God (v. 16), and *that purpose will not be thwarted!* What are the implications?

- "From now on we regard no one from a worldly point of view" (v. 16). Once even Jesus seemed a mere man; now we know better. The worldly point of view measures appearances and performance. We look beyond these to the work begun by God in the heart.

- "If anyone is in Christ, he is a new creation; the old has gone, the new has come" (v. 17). There may be no outward changes for a time, but in Christ there *is* an inner reality that guarantees transformation.

As an agent of the reconciliation God has accomplished in Christ, Paul now has a message. Step out and *experience* what Jesus has won! (v. 20).

See it? Paul expressed continuing confidence in the Corinthians because he *was* confident. He knew that, as men and women who had received new life from Jesus, they *would* grow and change.

Paul believed in them.

Because he believed in God.

## AN EXAMPLE
*2 Corinthians 8–9*

We can hardly overestimate the impact of Paul's teaching discussed just above. As parents, as pastors, as leaders, as members in the Body of Christ, we can honestly have confidence in the young. In spite of evidence to the contrary, we can *know* that they will grow. Secure in this knowledge, communicating our confidence and love, God will use us in a ministry of *reconciliation to believers,* stimulating and encouraging them to step out in expectant confidence and follow the Lord.

In these last two chapters of the section we're considering this week, we see a test case. We see a demonstration of how Paul carefully avoided the worldly ways of attempting to motivate and relied instead on the principles we have seen. These, with teaching, are all that any of us need.

*Giving in the church.* In the New Testament church of this time, there were no buildings to finance, no curriculums or programs to support. Yet there were needs within the body. Characteristically, these were "people needs." Funds were given to the apostles and others to support their ministries. When brothers were sick or in need, the rest of the family cared for them. When a natural disaster came, such as a famine, believers everywhere sent aid and relief.

This was not called "giving" then. Instead, the Greek word was *koinonia*, which means "sharing." As all of life was shared within the body, so were financial and material resources.

This has always been hard for us. Even in the first days of the church, Ananias and Sapphira found it difficult to let go of material possessions. It must have been difficult for the Corinthians, too. They were so accustomed to measuring by "what is seen" (4:18)! Yet, in these chapters Paul wrote to encourage them to share their material possessions with their brothers. His whole method was a demonstration of the revolutionary approach to motivation explained in this letter. There were no pledges here. No passing of offering plates with urgent appeals. No "buy a brick for the new building" campaigns. No giant thermometers on the front of the church with red satin ribbons to creep upward toward a campaign goal. No every-member canvasses.

Paul seemed to have found another way.

*Analysis.* I want you to have the excitement of personal discovery as you study this passage. So rather than go into detail, let me just point out a few elements of Paul's approach:

- Paul presented the need to be met.

- Paul encouraged the Corinthians to evaluate their own needs in view of their possessions and the situation of their brothers.
- Paul did *not* command; he wanted the giving to be done freely, with no external constraints.
- Paul presented truths that freed the believers to respond generously. (For instance, the fact that we cannot outgive God—9: 8.)

You'll no doubt find additional elements as well. And in the process you'll develop that special kind of confidence Paul knew.

Confidence in yourself.
Confidence in others.
Confidence based securely in God.

## GOING DEEPER

*to personalize*

1. Read 2 Corinthians 5—9 quickly, putting a check mark beside expressions of love and an *x* beside expressions of confidence. Then go back and examine these closely.

2. If you're a parent, think of a problem your child has. How have you been trying to help him grow beyond it? How has your discipline been *like* or *unlike* the pattern Paul sketches here?

3. Look back on your own childhood. How did your parents seek to motivate you? What impact do you believe their approach has had on your personality? (For instance, do you feel confident? Do you have a sense of self-worth, a good self-image?)

4. Study 2 Corinthians 8—9 *very closely.*

A.—List everything you note about Paul's approach to motivating the Corinthians to give.
B.—Can you see how the two principles in the chapter (unconditional love and expectant confidence) are expressed in Paul's approach here?
C.—Do you see any additional principles in these two chapters that might also be factors in motivation?

5. Imagine that you are chairman of your local church's finance committee. Develop a plan to present to the church board, based on principles you believe are expressed in this chapter.

6. List possible objections to your plan (5 above), and prepare your answers to them.

7. Pick someone you believe God might wish to use you to motivate. Plan carefully how you might follow Paul's principles to encourage, motivate, and "reconcile."

# 13
*2 Corinthians 10–13*

# THE USE AND ABUSE OF AUTHORITY

*AUTHORITY* IS SUCH A DIFFICULT WORD. We use it in so many ways.
- An encyclopedia is cited when someone asks, "What's your authority for that statement?"
- Professor so-and-so is introduced as an "authority on cybernetics."
- "Where's your search warrant?" is a demand for evidence of authority.
- "By the authority vested in me, I now pronounce you husband and wife."

Yet in our culture, the idea of authority has many negative connotations. To many, and especially to the young adult, authority tends to imply control, restriction, coercion, and impersonal command. *Authority* and *authoritarian* have become almost synonymous, and it is difficult for us to imagine how we might exercise authority without somehow asserting our right to control and command.

No wonder spiritual leadership and authority are

so misunderstood. No wonder the parent's authority over the child is so distorted—twisted by adult and young person alike. No wonder men called to lead the Church of God and given His authority for that task are troubled and uncertain. No wonder both often resort to a worldly approach to the exercise of authority—and stimulate rebellion rather than response.

## PAUL'S APPROACH

We may not be aware of it as we read 2 Corinthians, but it's true that in this letter the apostle was exercising his authority.

We're not likely to realize it because Paul didn't even mention authority until chapter 10. His second and final mention didn't come until near the end of this letter, in chapter 13. In both places he gave us a definition of the purpose of authority in the Body of Christ. It was something given to Paul by the Lord "for building you up rather than pulling you down" (10:8; see also 12:10). How much he hoped, as he closed this letter, that when he visited he would not be forced to "be harsh in my use of authority" (13:10).

We think of authority as something essentially harsh. But in the Body of Christ, the use of authority is marked by a distinct gentleness. Even the Corinthians missed the authority in the apostle's approach. Deceived again by their old way of understanding, they could not grasp why the apostle did not insist and command and demand. "Why," they must have wondered, "doesn't this leader *lead?*" They mistook Paul's wisdom for weakness.

> By the meakness and gentleness of Christ, I appeal to you—I, Paul, who am "timid" when face to face with you, but "bold" when away! I beg you that when I come I may not have to be as bold as I expect to be toward some people who think that we live by the standards of this world. For though we live in the world, we do not wage war as the world does. The weapons we fight with are not the weapons of the world. On the contrary, they have divine power to tear down strongholds. We demolish arguments and every pretension that sets itself up against the knowledge of God, and we take captive every thought to make it obedient to Christ.
> *2 Corinthians 10:1-5*

God's approach to authority operates on divine power. Through God's methods, Paul would be successful in taking "captive every thought" and making it "obedient to Christ."

What are some of those methods? Listen.

- "Not that we lord it over your faith, but we work with you for your joy" (1:24).
- "I urge you, therefore, to reaffirm your love for him" (2:8).
- "In every way we show ourselves to be servants of God" (6:4).
- "Dear friends, let us purify ourselves from everything that contaminates body and spirit, and let

us strive for perfection out of reverence for God" (7:1).
- "I am not commanding you, but I want to test the sincerity of your love" (8:8).
- "Here is my advice about what is best for you" (8:10).
- "Was it a sin for me to lower myself in order to elevate you?" (11:7.)

And the freedom Paul found to exercise his authority in such a gentle way was rooted both in his knowledge that this *is* God's way to use authority, and also in the knowledge that it was *God* who exercised authority through him.

> On my return I will not spare those who sinned earlier or any of the others, since you are demanding proof that Christ is speaking through me. He is not weak in dealing with you, but is powerful among you.
>
> 2 *Corinthians 13:2-3*

## AUTHORITY PRINCIPLES

The issue of spiritual authority is complex and important enough to warrant an entire book, not just part of a chapter. But this sketch of several basic characteristics may help give some perspective and also sensitize you to grasp more clearly what is behind the last intimate chapters of this most personal of epistles.

*Source.* Spiritual authority, unlike secular authority, is not rooted in position. An officer in the army or the president of a corporation has authority by virtue of his office. Spiritual authority, however (even though it may be associated with an office in the church or one's position as a parent), is actually rooted in one's *gift*. Paul relied on "the authority the Lord gave me" (13:10) in his dealings with the Corinthians.

This is important to grasp. If our authority is truly given us by the Lord, then He will be responsible for authenticating it! This is why Paul could say to those who were demanding proof that Christ was speaking through him, "*He* is not weak in dealing with you" (13:3). Jesus will vindicate the authority He has given.

*Goal.* Paul made it very clear that the purpose or goal of spiritual authority is to "build up." His authority was exercised purposefully: that by using all the spiritual weapons in God's arsenal, he might "take captive every thought to make it obedient to Christ" (10:5).

A very important concept is expressed here. It is *Jesus* who is Head of the Church. And He is the head of every man. The spiritual leader does not use his authority to bring believers to obey himself. Instead, spiritual authority is always exercised to lead the local body and each individual to obey Christ. The spiritual leader is not to attempt to exercise control over others; instead, he seeks to free them to be responsive to Jesus.

There are a number of reasons why this concept is vital. Authority that seeks to *control* focuses on externals. A person can "exercise authority" to manipulate or control another person's behavior through all the secular motivation methods we looked at in the last chapter. One reason why these methods are so often adopted in the church is that they are successful! But only if success is measured by conformity. It is true that many leadership methods are adapted to produce certain kinds of achievement. Using them, we can raise money, build bigger buildings, increase attendance in Sunday school. But the one thing such methods cannot do is to produce *commitment.* Commitment is a change within the human personality, an aspect of transformation. Commitment comes as a person freely chooses to respond to God.

All this underlies Paul's statement that authority had been given him to "build up." Rather than gain control over others, his exercise of authority was designed to free them to choose God's way willingly. This thought also finds expression in Paul's confident assertion that "Christ's love compels us" (5:14). It was the reality of Christ within, not external pressures, that Paul relied on to motivate believers to respond to the Lord.

*Relationships.* Paul has also, in relinquishing any claim to a supposed right to control, helped us to see more clearly the pattern of relationship appropriate to spiritual leadership. Paul did more than hint when he spoke of meekness and gentleness and insisted to the Corinthians that he would not "lord it over your faith" (1:24) but would instead "lower myself in order to elevate you" (11:7).

Rather than be relationally *over* others, the one

# REGIONS BEYOND

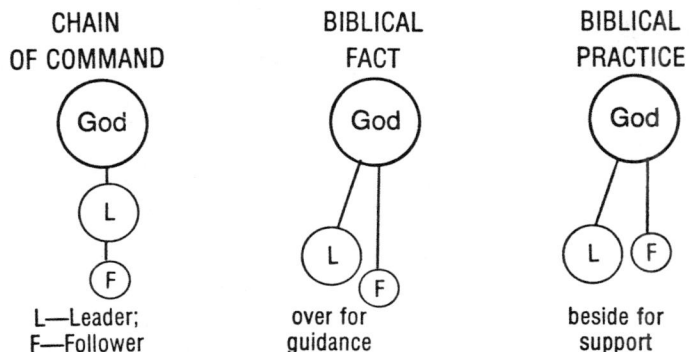

with spiritual authority takes his place beside them and thus lifts them up.

Perhaps we can diagram the correct and incorrect concepts this way:

The typical "chain of command" diagram represents the leader or parent as *between* God and the person under his authority. It is the same kind of chart used in military or business (or church) organizations to indicate lines of control and responsibility. This diagram seriously distorts the biblical picture.

An appropriate charting actually requires two diagrams. The first represents the *fact* of authority. While the leader *is* "above," and the other is "under" his authority, the leader is *not between the individual and God.* Instead, both the leader and the follower recognize Christ's lordship over each of them and over both of them together.

The fact of authority does admit the right of the

leader to lead, but it denies the right of the leader to control. Instead, the leader's influence flows from the reality of his *gift* and from the fact that, as one who has experienced significant growth and transformation, he can serve as an example and function as a teacher.

But even this chart is inadequate to represent how the leader *exercises* authority. We need another diagram for this, one that shows the leader choosing to humble himself, even to "lower myself in order to elevate you." How did Paul lower himself?

He requested rather than ordered. He gave advice rather than commands. He shared his weaknesses and thus took a stand beside men and women who knew themselves to be weak. He refused to "lord it over your faith," even when their worldly authorities made them critical of Paul's shameful lack of "boldness"!

The characteristics they associated with leadership were as foreign to true spiritual leadership as are those same traits with which we associate it today. But Jesus shows us an entirely new way:

> You know that the rulers of the Gentiles lord it over them, and their high officials exercise authority over them. Not so with you. Instead, whoever wants to become great among you must be your servant, and whoever wants to be first must be your slave—just as the Son of Man did not come to be served, but to serve, and to give his life a ransom for many.
>
> *Matthew 20:25-27*

*Attitude.* What is the appropriate attitude of the leader? A servant attitude. A servant who sees others, not himself, as important. A servant who humbles himself, concerned only with doing his master's will. A servant who willingly sets aside every outward symbol of power and relies completely on the power of God within the men and women he leads to stimulate response.

## EMBARRASSING

It almost seems embarrassing to read the words Paul writes in these last chapters of his letter. We're almost ashamed for him as he speaks out of the intensity of his love and pain. He seems almost . . . well, weak.

And yet, Paul was strong. Strong in God's way. "For Christ's sake, I delight in weaknesses, in insults, in hardships, in persecutions, in difficulties. For when I am weak, then I am strong" (2 Cor. 12:10). This was Paul's perspective. And it should become ours.

God's ways are not ours, and His thoughts are not ours. And our greatest need is to learn His ways.

## GOING DEEPER

*to personalize*

1. It is very difficult for us to grasp the implications of the Scripture's teaching on authority. Read 2 Corinthians 10—13 carefully, and if you wish, skim over the earlier chapters of this letter again.

Mark every section that gives you some insight into Paul's concept of or exercise of authority.

2. Working from the passages you marked, develop at least fifteen statements that you believe *do* reflect a biblical concept.

3. Then develop at least fifteen statements that you believe in some way distort the biblical concept.

4. Take a look at 2 Corinthians 10:6. What do you think this verse means?

*to probe*

1. What do you think are the most common misunderstandings of Paul's way of exercising authority? List them.

2. What answer would you give to each of the objections you've listed above? What passages of Scripture might you refer to in order to support your answer?

3. As a last study, write a biographical sketch of Paul. Write it as a member of the Corinthian church. Write either as someone who knew Paul from the beginning and was a supporter, describing not only Paul but your fellow believers' responses to him. Or write as a later convert, whose attitude toward Paul was initially antagonistic, but who gradually changed. This should be a "major" work! Shoot for eight to ten typed or handwritten pages.

4. Finally, record *on this page* the most important thing God has been doing in your life through this thirteen-week study of His Word.